HITLER'S GENERALS

HITLER'S GENERALS

Richard Humble

Doubleday & Company, Inc.
Garden City, New York
1974

Library of Congress Cataloging in Publication Data
Humble, Rjchard.
Hitler's Generals.
1. Hitler, Adolf, 1889-1945. 2. Generals—
Germany. 3. World War, 1939-1945—Germany. I. Title.
DD247.H5H83   1974   940.54'13'43
ISBN 0-385-03204-8
Library of Congress Catalog Card Number 73-20515

CONTENTS

CONTENTS

ILLUSTRATIONS

ACKNOWLEDGEMENTS

We should like to thank the following for permission to reproduce the photographs: Paul Popper for photographs 1, 2, 4, 8, 10 and 16; Ullstein Bilderdienst for the photograph of General Beck; Barnaby's Picture Library for photographs 6 and 7; Keystone Picture Library for photographs 5 and 12; the Mansell Collection for photographs 9 and 13; Camera Press for photographs 11 and 15.

Part I
FOUNDATION

FOUNDATION

Gröfaz (as the sardonic Berliners preferred to put it) was a contraction of *Der Grösster Feldherr aller Zeiten* – the greatest general of all time. And this was how Adolf Hitler fancied himself best. In trying to prove that he was right, he led to complete disaster the Germany he had reforged, and ended up by shooting himself in his own Supreme Headquarters beneath the ruins of Berlin. The very completeness of Germany's defeat in 1945 would seem by any reasonable standards to indicate Hitler's total lack of fitness for the sole command of the German armed forces – the Wehrmacht. There are plenty of facts to underline the case for the prosecution. Hitler rode roughshod over his professional military advisers. He took risks which never had the remotest chances of coming off. His obstinacy condemned hundreds of thousands of his soldiers to unnecessary deaths. And he lost his war.

But losing is not the final criterion when assessing generals, and never can be. It leaves too many questions unanswered. Napoleon lost to Wellington at Waterloo, but this does not make Wellington, *de facto,* the better general. It certainly does not make Wellington's army the better one – he said so himself at the time, in no uncertain terms. The two commanders only met in battle once, and when they did they were poles apart as far as their form was concerned. By medical standards alone, the Napoleon of Waterloo in 1815 was not the Napoleon of Austerlitz in 1805.

By the same token, the Hitler who cowered in the Berlin *Führerbunker* in 1945, a physical and mental wreck in a world of his own, was very far from being the Hitler who had directed the conquest of Poland, Denmark, Norway, Holland, Belgium, France, Yugoslavia, Greece, and western Russia. For every one of Hitler's myriad faults as a military commander there can be found strokes of brilliance which cannot be ignored. By backing the most modern ideas on armoured warfare – and doing it, be it noted, by listening to subordinates and giving them their heads – Hitler entitled himself to the credit for creating the Wehrmacht's Panzer force. Unhappy with the Army High Command's plan for the assault on the West in 1940, Hitler leaped at the alternative idea put forward by Manstein and backed it to the hilt, the result being the breakthrough at Sedan, the thrust to the Channel, and the fall of France. Ignoring the warnings of his admirals, Hitler insisted on the return to Germany through the English Channel of *Scharnhorst, Gneisenau,* and *Prinz Eugen.* He argued that the British would never be able to react fast enough and he was absolutely correct : the ships got through. And this from the man who is usually dismissed as the ultimate 'land animal', totally devoid of any understanding of naval matters.

Getting control of the Army was one of the most critical of Hitler's objectives during his rise to absolute mastery of Germany, for the Army had always had a dominant position in the Prussian state. This had been by no means diminished by the collapse of the German Empire in 1918 and the strike-ridden years of the 1920s. By the time Hitler appeared on the scene as a serious contender for top political honours, the German Army was a super-institution.

The first Hohenzollern kings of Prussia had made their top priority the maintenance of a strong standing army. They put it on a pedestal as the most important area of state service and earmarked the lion's share of their national revenues for it. Then came Frederick the Great and the epic years of war when Prussia held out only because of her formidable efforts in the field. When Frederick died in 1786, however, the Army stagnated. Obviously no improvement could be made to the military system which had been such a magnificent weapon in the hands of *Der alte Fritz*, and there was no need even to consider any of the new military fads which were being toyed with by armies such as the French.

The result was the appalling national collapse of 1806, when the fossilized descendant of Frederick the Great's army rolled ponderously out to put a stop to Napoleon's goings-on with the good old tactics. Napoleon and his Marshals pulverized the main Prussian field army in the double battle of Jena-Auerstädt on 14 October and by 6 November the whole kingdom had been overrun. On that date the last Prussian garrison to hold out – in Lübeck – laid down its arms. The Prussia of Frederick the Great had been totally and utterly defeated. It was the biggest disaster in Prussian history until the collapse of 1918.

For Prussia, the 1806 disaster was followed by six years of jumping to Napoleon's bidding as a carefully-watched trusty of the Grand Empire. It was from Berlin that Napoleon issued his famous decrees for a European blockade of English trade. Prussian troops marched with the *Grande Armée* when Russia was invaded in 1812. But by the time it became expedient for Prussia to go over to the Allied camp after Napoleon's Russian fiasco, vital changes had been made to the Prussian Army by the great reformers, Generals Scharnhorst and Gneisenau.

The reforms of 1806-13 had one aim and one aim alone: to expedite Prussia's recovery when the time came by raising a large army as quickly as possible. (By order of Napoleon the Prussian Army was cut back to 42,000 after Jena and Auerstädt.) What Scharnhorst and Gneisenau did for the Prussian state was to throw away the old eighteenth-century concept of a standing army of an agreed size, an élite force which was the largest item on the national budget. Beginning with the schools as the first natural outlet of militarist propaganda, they established a tradition of state-inspired incitement to military service. The reforms made Prussia (and the German Empire when proclaimed in 1871) the most successful nation in the world at making its subjects want to get into uniform.

This national mania, once created in Germany, was by no means dispelled by Germany's military defeat in the First World War. It survived, and it was meat and drink to the Nazis when they appeared on the scene in the 1920s. The shades of Scharnhorst and Gneisenau must have applauded rapturously when Alfred Rosenberg made his famous comment that what the Nazis wanted to see was 'all Germany in uniform and marching in columns'.

But before the Nazis reached the top and were really able to get organized – Hitler Youth, League of German Maidens, League of German Mothers, National Labour Corps, SA, SS, and all the rest of it – the German Army was the natural embodiment of this uniform mania. Its officers were gods. They got the best restaurant tables and theatre seats by divine right, not to mention automatic right of way on public thoroughfares. They were the élite. Their leaders regarded themselves as the defenders of German and Prussian tradition. Much more important, no political extremists had a hope of getting anywhere without their backing, and Hitler knew it.

Naturally one of his earliest ploys was ingratiating himself and his supporters with the Army, but Hitler's main trouble in the early days was that as a politician he was the youngest of men in the biggest of hurries. The crude, street-corner adolescence of Nazi tactics in the 1920s got an inevitable reaction from the Army : contempt. The greatest living German soldier, Field-Marshal von Hindenburg, was President of the German Republic, the Head of State, and his initial reaction to Hitler was as contemptuous as could be imagined. In election after election the Nazi Party proved that it was unable to get a decisive majority in the Reichstag by democratic means – but they were organized and they were persistent and their opponents were not. And the upshot was a spectacle which was the biggest natural piece of propaganda the Nazis had ever had : the great Hindenburg handing the Chancellorship of the German Republic to Hitler because none of Hitler's rivals could form a workable government.

Hitler became Chancellor on 30 January 1933. He could not have done it without the active collaboration of Colonel Oskar von Hindenburg, the old President's son – a dim and uninspired man who fancied himself as the 'power behind the throne'. After years of writing off the Nazis as an unsavoury gang of thugs, Oskar von Hindenburg came to the decision that the Nazis must be taken into the government after a *tête-à-tête* with Hitler on 22 January. In the tense forty-eight hours after the resignation of the last Chancellor, General Schleicher, on 28 January, the Army officer corps made its decision to endorse Hitler's accession to the Chancellorship. General Werner von Blomberg (who had been ousted from his post as second-in-command of the Army by Schleicher in 1930) was whisked back from the disarmament talks at Geneva, taken to the President by Oskar von Hindenburg, and sworn in as Defence Minister. Blomberg's brief was as simple as it was momentous for the course of German history : to see to it that the Army supported the new government, acting if necessary to put down any attempted *coup d'état* by force.

Three days after assuming the Chancellorship Hitler strengthened his position by holding a meeting with Blomberg, Army C-in-C Kurt von Hammerstein and Navy C-in-C Grand-Admiral Erich Raeder. These worthies listened in deep relief and approval as Hitler assured them that a National Socialist government would keep them out of politics and allow them to concentrate on expansion and rearmament for the defence of the state. Hitler certainly needed the compliance of the military chiefs because he was planning his next confrontation – tackling the Communists – and time was short. The meeting with Blomberg, Hammerstein and Raeder was on 2 February. The Reichstag went up in flames on 27 February. And the great 'Red peril' purge began within twenty-four hours. On 28 February the seven guarantees of individual and civil liberties in the German constitution were suspended 'for the protection of People and State'. And both Army and Navy swallowed the orgy of nation-wide bullying and intimidation which followed without so much as a murmur.

Having thus obtained the right to arrest any opposition leaders he chose, Hitler followed through with a splendid gesture of respect for the Army that went down very well indeed. This was the opening of the Reichstag – the first of the new régime – in the Potsdam Garrison Church. It was an inspired choice of venue, for the Garrison Church was, quite simply, the highest shrine of Prussian militarism, redolent with memories of Frederick the Great, Bismarck, and the glories of the Imperial Reich. The ceremony, held on 21 March, was stage-managed to the last detail by Goebbels and heaped lavish praise and votes of gratitude on Hindenburg as the incarnation of Germany's military heritage. And the innumerable press photographs taken of Hitler, looking extremely uncomfortable in morning dress, clasping hands with Hindenburg (resplendent in uniform full dress complete with *Pickelhaube)* got top display not only throughout Germany but outside as well. It was yet another stage in Hitler's ingratiation policy, to convince doubtful German voters that the Nazis were *the* party to support.

Exploiting his new moral victory with characteristic speed, Hitler passed his 'Enabling Act' through the Reichstag within forty-eight hours after the Potsdam ceremony (23 March). The Act was a five-paragraph voluntary acceptance of dictatorship, placing supreme power in the hands of the Reich Cabinet for a four-year period. Solemn pledges that the 'position' of the President and Reichstag would remain unchanged were duly swallowed and the Act was passed by 441 votes to 84. This was how Hitler became dictator – by constitutional means. The next stage was the elimination of all rival political parties to leave only one party – the Nazis – in Germany. The Social Democrats went on 22 June, the National Party followed on 29 June and the Bavarian People's Party on 4 July. On 14 July the decree went out that 'The National Socialist German Worker's Party constitutes the only political party in Germany.'

It was the constitutional nature of the Nazi revolution which made it virtually impossible for the Army to object or intervene – even if it had been so inclined after the assiduous buttering-up to which it had been subjected. But the next stage in Hitler's programme vitally affected the Army: Hitler's settling of accounts with Ernst Röhm and the SA storm trooper thugs.

Röhm and the SA had been the strong-arm boys of the Nazi movement right from the start. Bullying and intimidation were their stock-in-trade and the achievement of revolution by violence was their ideal. In 1933 Röhm regarded himself not only as the architect of Hitler's victory : he saw himself as the future leader of a new German army based on an expanded SA, with himself as commander. This would be a national army and he would be its Bonaparte. Hitler, naturally, had other ideas.

At Nuremberg on 23 September Hitler began to put his cards on the table *vis-à-vis* the pretensions of the SA.

'On this day [he announced] we should particularly remember the part played by our Army, for we all know well that if, in the days of our revolution, the Army had not stood on our side, then we should not be standing here today. We can assure the Army that we shall never forget this, that we see in them the bearers of the tradition of our glorious old Army, and that with all our heart and all our powers we will support the spirit of this Army.'

In soliciting the Army's tacit support in the event of a showdown with Röhm and the SA, Hitler was not merely trying to preserve his existing powers : he was out to extend them still further. By the end of 1933 it was evident that the days of the frail and elderly Hindenburg were numbered. What would happen when the old President died? There were still plenty of old-time reactionaries who would be only too glad to see the Hohenzollern dynasty restored. Hitler knew what he wanted : the unchallenged position of head of state, with every soldier in the Army required to swear the oath of allegiance to him. As ever, he needed the consent of the armed forces' high commands to reach this new goal – and he got it.

The deal was settled aboard the pocket-battleship *Deutschland* on 11 April 1934. *Deutschland* was sailing from Kiel to Königsberg for the spring manoevres in East Prussia, and on board were Hitler, Blomberg, Raeder and the Commander-in-Chief of the Army, General Freiherr von Fritsch. Hitler offered them a straight bargain. If the forces backed him as Hinden-

burg's successor, he would guarantee that the SA would be put
in its place and reduced to impotence, and the Army and Navy
confirmed as the official arms-bearers of the Reich. Hitler had
no trouble in getting Raeder's acceptance there and then, but
von Fritsch insisted on calling a conference of his top generals
before giving his answer. This was done at Bad Nauheim on
16 May and the Army reacted unanimously in accepting
Hitler's offer.

On 23 March 1933 the Reichstag had handed over its con-
stitutional prerogatives to Hitler by passing the Enabling Act.
Now the Army and the Navy, by agreeing to the 'Pact of the
Deutschland', had done the same.

The axe came down on 30 June 1934 – the notorious 'Blood
Purge' wiped out the SA leaders and broke the organization
as an independent force in being. The purge was given rubber-
stamp approval in the form of messages of congratulation from
Hindenburg and Blomberg, but they ignored the fact that two
generals had been assassinated in the purge. These were former
Chancellor Schleicher and his friend, Kurt von Bredow, both
of whom were shot down by murder squads of the other Nazi
private army – Heinrich Himmler's SS. The German officer
corps made no protest at these two assassinations. Only two
Army VIPs spoke out against the murders of Schleicher and
von Bredow: First-World-War hero Field-Marshal von
Mackensen and former Army C-in-C Hammerstein. The
German Army had endorsed Nazi terror tactics by its silence.
And not for the last time.

The moment for the generals to keep their side of the
Deutschland bargain came with terrifying speed. Hindenburg
died on 2 August 1934 and the Presidency of the Reich was
vacant at last. Hitler and Goebbels had it all worked out. At
noon on the 2nd – a mere three hours after Hindenburg
breathed his last – a government announcement stated that a
law passed on the previous day had provided for the merging
of the offices of Chancellor and President. Adolf Hitler was
now *Führer* – 'Leader' (as he was already referred to by the
Party) – and Chancellor of the German Reich, and Commander-in-Chief of the armed forces to boot. The wording of

the new oath of allegiance to be taken by all servicemen had been prepared. It read :

'I swear by God this sacred oath, that I will render uncon-ditional obedience to Adolf Hitler, the Führer of the German Reich and people, Supreme' Commander of the Armed Forces, and will be ready as a brave soldier to risk my life at any time for this oath.'

From now on every officer and man in the German armed forces who took this oath pledged his personal fealty to the Nazi regime, and to its embodiment in Hitler himself. Second thoughts about what the government was doing – let alone active criticism – could now only be described in one way : treason. To have duped the armed forces into putting them-selves into such a position was Hitler's master-stroke. From August 1934 the Army was legally *his*, body and soul, from private up to general.

Just what sort of an army was it ?

When the hated *'Diktat'* of Versailles was forced on Germany after the First World War the victorious Allies saw it as a hammer which would keep Germany permanently stunned. She was to be territorially contained, forbidden warplanes and submarines, and the strength of her Army and Navy was to be reduced to the minimum. The maximum laid down for the postwar German Army – the *Reichswehr* – was 100,000 men. On paper these should have been crippling limitations, but only on paper, for the Allied hammer did not stun : it forged new and much more formidable weapons instead.

With the former military machine dismantled by the Allied *'Diktat'* the commanders of the German Army and Navy were given the bare minimum of material with which to work, but at the same time they were given a clean sheet. They were largely cut free from all the deficiencies which lived on and flourished in the Allied armies. The German skeleton forces, in other words, were ideal test-beds for new ideas, and were never regarded as anything but nuclei for future expan-sion. In short the period after Versailles was exactly like the period after Jena in the Napoleonic Wars, as far as the German armed forces were concerned. This time, however, the rôles of Scharnhorst and Gneisenau were performed by one man : Colonel-General Hans von Seeckt.

Seeckt took over command of the *Reichswehr* in 1920. Since the Armistice the Army's morale had suffered heavily during the mutinies, strikes and riots in the Fatherland, and Seeckt's first task was to restore the self-respect of the officer corps. His basic programme was two-fold : to keep the Army out of politics and train it *à la* Scharnhorst for better and bigger things in the future. And the *Leitmotiv* of the Seeckt regime was the training of future commanders, right the way down the line – grooming corps commanders for army command, divisional commanders for corps command, and so on down to the lowliest lieutenant.

Seeckt's concept of the *Führerheer* – an 'army of leaders' – stopped short of training all senior NCOs for commissioned rank. There was much opposition to this, for the Reichswehr officers of the 1920s were all ex-Imperial officers and a formidable mass of reactionary thinking still blocked most modern or excessively far-sighted ideas at source. Officer selection from the ranks was not to be generally accepted until the late 1930s. What Seeckt's *Reichswehr* did achieve, however, was NCO training second to none. The soldiers of the 'hundred-thousand-man army' who had made the rank of sergeant by the early 1930s were one hundred per cent professionals and the backbone of Hitler's new Wehrmacht.

Seeckt's constant preoccupation was bending the rules of Versailles, and the most important success in this field was the research work put in on motorized and armoured forces. This created the raw materials for the Wehrmacht's first Panzer divisions in the 1930s. Heinz Guderian (of whom more later) was deeply involved in these experiments and his memoirs contain deeply-revealing references to the reactionary opposition to be found in the Reichswehr under Seeckt and after. When he tried to get hold of some transports for troop-carrying in 1924 he was told 'To hell with combat! They're supposed to carry flour!' And in 1931, from the Inspector of Transport Troops : 'You're too impetuous. Believe me, neither of us will ever see German tanks in operation in our lifetime.' Then in 1933, from Chief of the General Staff General Ludwig Beck : 'No, no, I don't want to have anything to do with you people. You move too fast for me.'

At Versailles the Allies believed that they had struck a deadly blow at Prussian militarism by ordering the dissolution of the German General Staff. Seeckt managed to keep it in being, and although Hitler paid the usual lip-service to its glorious traditions he was disappointed and resentful. The General Staff was another autonomous body which he must always handle with care, and in his first two years of power all went well. But the General Staff was always one of Hitler's pet hates, and not only because he knew very well that originally the Army regarded him as a jumped-up corporal. As a genuine, embittered veteran of the trenches to whom the defeat of 1918 had come as a shattering blow, Hitler never stopped 'cursing the Staff for incompetent swine'. And the whole macabre story of Hitler and his generals is based on the fact that between 1934 and 1939 the generals were proved wrong whenever they forecast disaster, while Hitler's plans were triumphantly proved right.

Even before the Army's fears about the future of the SA were assuaged by the 'Blood Purge' of 30 June 1934, the Nazi pay-off had begun. Blomberg and Fritsch had already been given Hitler's official go-ahead for the expansion of the Army from 100,000 to 300,000 by October 1934. He had, in fact, begun to 'open the toy cupboard', as Alan Clark has put it. And on 16 March 1935 Hitler formally announced general rearmament, military conscription, a thirty-six division army half a million strong, and the existence of the new air force, the Luftwaffe. On the following day – *Heldengedenktag* (Heroes' Remembrace Day) – the new *Wehrmacht* commanders turned out for the ceremony (which was stage-managed with the usual imposing trappings) amid national rejoicing. The Führer had given Germany her honour back ; the shackles of Versailles had been broken.

And the generals had been given their biggest bouquet yet. Erich von Manstein, the future star general of the Russian campaign, was a staff officer in the Berlin 3rd Military District in March 1935, and he later testified at Nuremberg that if the General Staff had been consulted it would have proposed no more than twenty-one divisions. Now Hitler had given the Army no less than thirty-six. Fulsome thanks were rendered to the Führer on that memorable *Heldengedenktag* by Blomberg in a somewhat nauseating speech, in which he claimed that it was to the Army's credit, 'removed from political conflict', that foundations had been laid down 'on which a God-given architect could build'.

The inevitable sequel to the announcements of 16 March 1935 could only be the military reoccupation of the Rhineland, which had been decreed a demilitarized zone by the terms of Versailles. But sending troops across the Rhine would be a very different matter from making speeches in Berlin. If the French Army moved in to check the reoccupation, a full-scale international crisis must ensue and the still small German Army would not stand a chance if this resulted in a showdown.

It was with the Rhineland *coup* that Hitler's absolute control of the generals, proving them wrong and himself absolutely right, was established for the first time. In any event the General Staff knew very well that the Rhineland must be reoccupied. It was the only way in which Germany – rearmed to the teeth or not – could get her guard up properly to counter an invasion from the west. It was just that they could not see how they could possibly get away with it. Nevertheless, planning started from 2 May 1935 under the code-word '*Schülung*'. And it was while the details were being thrashed out that Colonel Alfred Jodl, head of the Home Defence Department, first emerged in the counsels of the German High Command.

Although he had briefed Blomberg and the Army strategists to prepare for an operation which must be carried out 'at lightning speed', Hitler dragged his feet throughout the summer, autumn and winter of 1935. He was waiting to see how matters went with the new Franco-Soviet mutual assistance pact, signed in March but not yet ratified by the French Parliament. Another interesting test-case which needed studying was the aftermath of the latest defiance of the League of

Nations: Mussolini's invasion of Abyssinia, launched in October. The League reacted by decreeing sanctions against Italy. Only partially enforced, these sanctions neatly demolished all extant goodwill between Italy on the one hand and France and Britain on the other; they certainly did nothing whatever to help the Abyssinians, and all this was cheering news to Hitler. Finally, on 27 February 1936, the French Parliament finally ratified the pact with Soviet Russia – and Hitler took the plunge.

The demilitarized Rhineland was entered at dawn on 7 March. The German forces involved were tiny: only one division for the whole of the Rhineland, with three battalions pushing across the Rhine to Aachen, Trier, and Saarbrücken. As a military venture it was the most colossal piece of cheek, and Blomberg's nerve was the first to crack. As he left the Reichstag (which predictably had roared hysterical approval of Hitler's announcement of the reoccupation), Blomberg's face was seen to be white and twitching. He was not the only one. Hitler himself later confessed that the ensuing forty-eight hours were the most nerve-racking of his life, but his immediate follow-up boast that only his iron nerves had saved the situation was nothing but the truth. Unable to believe that the French were actually going to sit tight, Jodl and Blomberg pressed for a withdrawal of the troops west of the Rhine when France's General Gamelin timidly shifted thirteen divisions to reinforce the Maginot Line. The French hesitated and the British looked the other way and gradually the combined blood-pressure of the German General Staff began to drop. It was true. The Führer had been right.

All in all, 1936 was a good year for the dictators. In Abyssinia Mussolini's forces took Addis Ababa; the League of Nations finally gave up and dropped its sanctions against Italy. The Berlin-Rome 'Axis' – a joint agreement of common policy – was announced. General Franco's rebellion in Spain gained rapid ground and established a third unfriendly dictatorship on France's borders. Germany and Japan signed the Anti-Comintern Pact. By 30 January 1937 Germany's position at home and abroad was the strongest since 1914. On the fourth anniversary of his accession to power, Hitler could claim that it was all his doing, and he did. But what had been achieved was only a beginning.

The year 1937 was a deceptive interlude of peace, humming with preparations for war. The German Wehrmacht continued to expand in all three of its branches: Army (*Heer*), Navy (*Kriegsmarine*), and Air Force (*Luftwaffe*). But it was only an interlude, and could be nothing more. Hitler now had his sights set on the big time, and he knew very well that his next objectives would not be like marching into the Rhineland. They would in all probability result in all-out war in Europe; and on 5 November 1937 he called his commanders to the Reich Chancellery and told them so.

At that historic meeting which, despite all subsequent academic quibbling on the subject, roughed out the blueprint for the coming of the Second World War, Hitler used a new technique on his military commanders: blinding them with science. For hours they had to sit and listen to him rambling on, spouting reams of economic jargon which, as Hitler always said with a fair degree of accuracy, was often forgotten by generals. He sketched out his plan for a self-supporting German Reich which would embrace every German on the Continent. This, he stated, was his life's crusade. But tremendous strategic advantages would also accrue to Germany. All the frontier weaknesses outstanding from Versailles would be eradicated – the isolation of East Prussia, bitten off from the Reich by the 'Polish Corridor' and the Free City of Danzig, the long, vulnerable arc of the Pomeranian-Silesian frontier with Poland, and the deep, wedge-like salient of the Czech frontier. Austria must be welded to the Reich. The racial Germans in the Czech Sudentenland must be restored to their heritage and Czechoslovakia destroyed as an independent state. Then it would be time to settle accounts with Poland.

Hitler had weighed all the implications. He was, he stated quite bluntly, 'resolved on war'.

But for once the Generals – Blomberg and Fritsch – answered him back, arguing against the folly of risking all the current gains by taking on too much with too little. They were

supported by the Foreign Minister, Neurath. Hitler ignored
them to a man, but as the meeting broke up one thing was clear
in his mind : before he made his next international move the
obstructive elements must be weeded out and his control over
the armed forces strengthened still more. There was still the
chance that they might combine against him.

As before, no time was wasted. Neurath, Blomberg and
Fritsch had to go, and they went quickly. Blomberg proved the
easiest to axe. In January 1938 he married his secretary.
Unfortunately for him she turned out to be a former prostitute,
and a great storm of moral indignation blew up which would
have done credit to a Victorian officers' mess. (Raeder sent an
officious young lieutenant to call on Blomberg and demand
that he divorce his new wife for the honour of the officer corps.
Raeder's envoy delivered not only the message but a loaded
pistol. Blomberg rejected both.) Hitler sacked Blomberg on 25
January, and the post of Defence Minister and Commander-in-
Chief of the Wehrmacht was vacant.

Meanwhile Himmler and his SS sleuths had been putting the
finishing touches to a monstrous frame-up job for the downfall
of Fritsch. This was far better box-office than Blomberg's *faux
pas* : a formal charge that Fritsch had been guilty of homo-
sexual relations, with unsavoury false witnesses at hand to
swear to it. Fritsch was held in the highest respect by the
military and this monumental lie was a devastating blow to the
morale of the officer corps. This should, in fact, have been the
moment when the German officer corps finally made up its
mind that the Nazi regime had gone too far, and thrown it out.
But things worked out differently because Hitler played his
cards very cleverly indeed.

Fritsch, having refused to answer the charge, was sent on
indefinite leave ; his demand that his honour be vindicated in
a military court was shelved. This demand was repeated by the
Chief of the Army General Staff, Ludwig Beck. And in the last
week of January 1938 an Army investigation committee –
working, be it noted, with the Ministry of Justice – had no
trouble in unearthing the facts behind the trumped-up charge
against Fritsch. The Army went so far as to take custody of all

key witnesses and demand a court martial to clear the name of
the Commander-in-Chief – publicly. How could Hitler and his
regime have survived the inevitable findings of such a court
without being permanently discredited?

Hitler, however, replied with another re-shuffle of power
which, as ever, worked in his favour and his favour alone. On
4 February 1938 he issued a new decree, and this was the
clincher.

Blomberg's successor was named : Hitler, who would now be
Commander-in-Chief of the Armed Forces, exercising direct
command in addition to his honorific title of Supreme Commander by virtue of being head of state. Blomberg's former
War Ministry was abolished. In its place appeared the High
Command of the Armed Forces – *Oberkommando der
Wehrmacht,* or OKW, with Hitler as its head. As Chief-of-Staff
for the OKW Hitler selected one of the worst yes-men in the
history of the German Army : Wilhelm Keitel, soon to be
known throughout the officer corps as *Lakeitel* (lackey).

It was announced that both Blomberg and Fritsch had
resigned 'for reasons of health', but Hitler was careful not to
overstep the mark when it came to replacing Fritsch. Once
again, he was able to exploit his generals' sex-lives, for his new
appointee, General Walther von Brauchitsch, was trying for a
divorce, and it was well known that his new *inamorata* was a
fanatical Nazi. Thus by helping along the progress of
Brauchitsch's divorce action, Hitler got himself a Commander-
in-Chief of the Army with a sense of personal obligation to the
regime, but it was not quite as simple as that. Hitler had picked
a candidate whose standing in the eyes of his brother officers –
divorce or no divorce – was high.

Furthermore, Hitler ordered sixteen top generals – army and
corps commanders – to be replaced. Another forty-four were
transferred from their current commands. Hitler then delighted
Hermann Göring (who had cherished hopes that he might be
appointed Blomberg's successor) by naming him Field-Marshal
and making him the top-ranking officer in Germany. In the
same package-deal of sackings and reappointments, Neurath
was replaced as Reich Foreign Minister by Joachim von

Ribbentrop, a vain and arrogant nonentity who was as big a toady as Keitel, but without the latter's professional training. The purge of the three conservatives who had talked back to Hitler when he had told them that he was 'resolved on war' was complete. And the Führer's control of the German war machine had been strengthened out of all measure.

Once again the officer corps swallowed all this, content with one promise : an official hearing for Fritsch, which was granted. But it was held in private with the brand-new Field-Marshal Göring as its President, supported on either hand by Brauchitsch and Raeder. And scarcely had the proceedings opened on 10 March when a far greater crisis broke upon the scene and eclipsed the whole business. Hitler had decided that the time had come for the annexation (*Anschluss*) of Austria.

The details of how the *Anschluss* was brought about are not relevant here. They form a four-year story of the creation of 'incidents' in Austria, which were trumpeted to the world by the Nazi press as the persecution of 'loyal Germans' whose only desire was to come 'home to the Reich'. The basic fact is that the takeover of Austria, which terrified the German generals as a straight military proposition far more than the reoccupation of the Rhineland had done, was achieved by gangster-style bluffing on one side and by the honest fear of civil war on the other. It is superfluous to define which side was which.

The hard bluffing started at an interview between Hitler and the Austrian Chancellor, Dr Schuschnigg, at Berchtesgaden on 4 February 1938. During day-long talks Hitler deluged Schuschnigg with an incessant cascade of abuse and neo-historical tripe : 'The whole history of Austria is just one un-mitigated act of high treason'; 'Every national idea was sabotaged by Austria throughout history'; and 'I am going to solve the so-called Austrian problem one way or the other.' The climax came when Hitler rushed to the door and bellowed 'General Keitel!' before dismissing Schuschnigg abruptly. Keitel came bustling in, only to be told by a chortling Hitler that there were no orders for him. 'I just wanted to have you here.'

The aftermath was the 'four weeks' agony', with Hitler step-

ping up the pressure on Schuschnigg to agree to the Nazifica-
tion of Austria. For a while it seemed that Schuschnigg would
yield – but then, on 9 March, the Austrian Chancellor
announced that the whole proposition would be put to the
Austrian people by plebiscite on 13 March. Was Austria to
remain independent – yes or no ? There were quite sufficient
Austrian nationalists to make the answer a foregone con-
clusion ; the prospect of a pro-*Anschluss* or anti-*Anschluss*
plebiscite was as frightening a prospect to Hitler as a public trial
of Fritsch would have been, the difference being that a public
Fritsch trial would have discredited him at home, whereas the
Austrian plebiscite bade fair to discredit him before the world.

The time had come, in fact, to prove whether there was anything in the scabbard but the hilt. And there was not.

In March 1938 only one plan existed for sending German
troops into Austria : 'Case Otto', armed intervention to prevent
the restoration of the Habsburg Prince Otto. Hitler ordered
'Case Otto' on Thursday 10 March, giving the Wehrmacht
forty-eight hours in which to move. But as Beck admitted at
the time, the 'Otto' file was empty : no preparations had been
made. Frenzied improvizations were made and mobilization
orders were sent out to the Luftwaffe and three Army corps on
the evening of the tenth, while Hitler had sent off a conciliatory
message to Mussolini asking the Duce to turn a blind eye to
German relations with Austria in the immediate future. Here
was no coldly calculated master-stroke, planned to the last
detail. It was frantic improvization, done completely off the
cuff, with disaster threatening if the French, the British, the
Czechs, or even Mussolini, reacted the wrong way, and with
the possibility of armed resistance from the Austrians thrown
in. No wonder the generals were appalled at the prospect. But
once again Hitler's nerves saved the day.

Everything clicked into place at the last minute. The French
were wallowing in political crisis; their Cabinet had resigned
on the tenth, and a new government was not formed until all
was up with Austria on the thirteenth. The British were swap-
ping Foreign Secretaries – Lord Halifax for Anthony Eden.
Mussolini told a delighted Hitler that Austria was no concern

of Italy's. Under pressure from the chief Nazi hatchet-man in Austria, Seyss-Inquart, Schuschnigg called off the plebiscite and resigned. And on 12 March, as the first editions of the Berlin newspapers were announcing that German Austria was being 'saved from chaos', the Wehrmacht crossed the frontier.

In *The Second World War,* Churchill has poured scorn on the performance of the German Army during the occupation of Austria, seeking to strengthen his case that Germany's neighbours were unbelievably feeble not to have recognized a paper tiger when they saw one. He refers in particular to the mass breakdowns which afflicted the armoured and mechanized forces of Heinz Guderian's Panzer units, which were now being given the chance to show what they could do. Guderian himself has pointed out that the whole operation had come as an immense surprise to one and all, and that in March 1938 the Panzer force had everything to learn about supplying and maintaining armoured and motorized units and keeping them on the move. He admits that breakdowns did occur, and that it was even necessary to arrange for the Austrian garage proprietors along the route to put their filling stations at the disposal of the 'liberating' Wehrmacht. (At this the mind certainly boggles, when one thinks of the smooth supply machine which kept the Panzers rolling in Poland, France, and Russia in the next thirty-six months.) But Guderian has shown, too, that the *psychological* impact of the appearance of armoured forces was appreciated and exploited to the full. Nothing is more ominous than a rattling, thundering armoured column on the move, and nationalist Austrians might well have panicked at the sight. Guderian, however, had his armoured vehicles festooned with greenery like ornamental Christmas trees, scrawled with patriotic slogans, with the crews lounging about on top grinning and waving to the people they passed on the road. This little trick did much to paper over the cracks in his force during the march into Austria.

Austria was declared a province of the Reich on 13 March. Hitler entered Vienna in triumph on the following day. And on 17 March the Fritsch trial – now reduced to complete unimportance by the events of the past week – was reopened. The affair was tidied up in under forty-eight hours and swept under the carpet; no public announcements. Fritsch was cleared; the SS frame-up was exposed, but no mention was made of Himmler's guilt. Nor did the Army get its former Commander-in-Chief back, despite the verdict. Fritsch soldiered on, however, in total obscurity, as Colonel-in-Chief of his old regiment, the 12th Artillery ; he went to war with it in September 1939 and dourly got himself killed in action on the twenty-second, during the siege of Warsaw. They brought him back and buried him in Berlin with full military honours. Fritsch had found, the hard way, that Hitler's incredible bloodless conquest of Austria had made many Germans forget a lot of things very quickly – especially among the generals of the officer corps.

A mighty '*Ja*' vote for the *Anschluss* sealed Hitler's triumph over Austria on 10 April. And on 21 April Hitler and Keitel commenced new discussions over the next victim – Czechoslovakia – under the code-name 'Case Green'.

After Germany's merger with Austria, Czechoslovakia was outflanked on three sides – but Czechoslovakia was a very different nut to crack, and the German generals knew it. The western frontier consisted of a natural bastion, formed by the Bohemian mountains, and their heights contained a tough facsimile of the Maginot Line with the most formidable of the latter's defences built in. The Czech Army was well armed and excellently equipped – its Skoda tanks were a match for any-thing the Germans had in 1938 – and it could mobilize a field army of 800,000 men (with a total call-up of a million). At the time this was almost exactly the combat strength of the Wehrmacht. If the French – let alone the Poles – could be induced to support Czechoslovakia, Germany would be out-matched in the field by three to one.

'Case Green' covered the overall scheme for taking Czecho-slovakia, and 'direct military action' was only a part of this. The idea was that the Reich would bide its time until inter-national tension – natural or deliberately manipulated – was at its most favourable pitch. But the final goal was put in black and white right from the start : 'to smash Czechoslovakia'. 'Smashing the Czechs' became a catch-phrase of Hitler's in

OKW documents dating from the months after the *Anschluss*. And it must be said that not one general raised any objection on moral grounds to the deliberate and premeditated destruction of Czechoslovakia. Strategically it would do the Reich a power of good, shortening her eastern frontier by hundreds of miles and adding excellent war industries and stocks of *materiel* to the German war machine. But – once again – how could Germany possibly expect the Western powers to look the other way ? Spokesman for the opposition on these grounds was Army Chief-of-Staff Ludwig Beck.

From May to July 1938, as Hitler and his OKW planners forged ahead with the refining of 'Case Green', Beck nagged away at Brauchitsch with a series of detailed, well-argued memoranda urging that the plan to tackle Czechoslovakia be rejected by the Army. Beck worked himself up to such a pitch that his last memorandum to Brauchitsch demanded that the Commander-in-Chief of the Army threaten Hitler with the mass resignation of the General Staff unless the plan was dropped. But, as mentioned above, Hitler had done a shrewd job when he appointed Brauchitsch to replace Fritsch. Beck found that Brauchitsch was a broken reed, and that his memoranda were being sat on. Only once did Brauchitsch venture to give Hitler a watered-down version of what Beck really wanted made clear – and Hitler's response was typical. On 10 August he held a generals' conference at Berchtesgaden – not of commanding generals, but their chiefs-of-staff – and gave them the full treatment, stressing how good the chances of 'Case Green' really were. To the protests of General Gustav von Wietersheim that the German 'Army of the West' could only field five divisions against the full striking strength of the French Army, Hitler bellowed : 'I say to you, *Herr General,* that the position will be held not only for three weeks but for three years !'

On 15 August, at a military review held at Jüterbog, Hitler announced to the Army generals that he was resolved to settle the Czech 'problem' by force. This time not a word was said. And three days later General Beck, embittered by the feeling that he had been betrayed not only by Brauchitsch but by his colleagues, resigned as Army Chief-of-Staff. He went about it

as Fritsch had done – without beating the drum in public – and
if he had expected that his resignation would trigger off a wave
of sympathetic resignations which must force the Führer to
think again, he was sadly mistaken. As the autumn of 1938
approached, Hitler's generals knew that 'Case Green' was going
forward and that a date had been set : 1 October. But they had
failed to stand together and stop Hitler from playing with fire
over Czechoslovakia.

Hitler's pretext for picking a fight with Czechoslovakia was
the Sudetenland – the area of territory across the Czech
frontier inhabited by racial Germans. As with the case of
Austria, the Nazis had set up a vociferous 'home to the Reich'
movement in the Sudetenland, which ensured that there would
be more than enough 'anti-German incidents' to denounce
piously in their newspapers. But Hitler was also fortunate in
that he was able to rope in Poland and Hungary when it came
to helping himself to Czechoslovak territory. Both countries
had nationalist claims of their own on Czechoslovakia :
Poland wanted the Teschen area, and Hungary wanted a big
slice of Slovakia plus Sub-Carpathian Ruthenia (the eastern
'tail' of Czechoslovakia). This meant that any challenge to a
German invasion of Czechoslovakia would have to come from
the Czechs themselves, France, and Britain – and in terms of
prompt military counter-action that ruled out Britain. France,
however, would not act alone unless Britain would back her up.
And neither France nor Britain were prepared to fight for
Czechoslovakia – Hitler's 'intuition' was 100 per cent correct.
In the cant phrase of this climate of appeasement, the official
Anglo-French line, when it came to the crunch, was that if war
must come it must be over far more serious issues than the
rights of Czechoslovakia to deny reasonable foreign claims on
her territory.

So it was that Hitler, determined to act on 1 October whatever happened, engineered the string of international crises
which ended by giving him all he wanted at Munich in September. Playing on the joint Anglo-French apprehension, he
manoeuvred Britain's Prime Minister Neville Chamberlain
into believing that a fair solution was up to the Czechs. But the

final betrayal at Munich, when Chamberlain, French Premier
Daladier, Mussolini, and Hitler signed the joint agreement
which sold out Czechoslovakia, was not reached before Europe
had come to the very brink of war. This happened after the
Hitler-Chamberlain talks at Bad Godesberg reached deadlock
on 22 September, and the ensuing crisis pushed even Hitler's
nerves to the limit. American journalist William Shirer saw
him at Godesberg on the morning of the twenty-second. 'He
seemed to have a peculiar tic. Every few steps he cocked his
right shoulder nervously, his left leg snapping up as he did so.
He had ugly, black patches under his eyes. He seemed to be, as
I noted in my diary that evening, on the eve of a nervous
breakdown.' But the generals were far more deeply affected.
They had formed a conspiracy and were determined to strike if
Hitler pushed Germany into war over the Sudetenland or any
other issue connected with Czechoslovakia. And nothing is
more deeply indicative of the desperate nature of the crisis of
September 1938 than this generals' conspiracy.

Since the birth of the Nazi regime in 1933 there had always
been a tiny core of resistance to it – but until the Sudeten crisis
of 1938 it had always been essentially civilian. Now men like
Ewald von Kleist, Karl Goerdeler, Fabian von Schlabrendorff,
Helmuth von Moltke, and their colleagues in impotent conspiracy found that the generals were willing to listen to their
plans to arrest Hitler, prevent war, and save Germany from
disaster. The two key generals were the deposed Beck (who was
held in equally high esteem outside and inside the Army) and
Beck's successor as Chief-of-Staff, Franz Halder. With them
were General Erwin von Witzleben, commanding the Berlin
military district; General Erich Höppner, commanding a
Panzer division in Thuringia; and General Heinrich von
Stülpnagel, Army High Command's quartermaster-general.
There was also Colonel Hans Oster, Chief-of-Staff of the OKW
Intelligence Bureau (the *Abwehr*). The plotters resolved that as
soon as Hitler gave the executive order to attack Czechoslo-
vakia he would be arrested by the Army and tried before a
People's Court. Military government would replace Nazi rule
and 'clean up' the Reich, eventually handing over power to a

democratic – and safely conservative – government.

Every single one of the conditions deemed essential by the plotters came about in the last week of September 1938. Diplomatic negotiations hung fire and Germany was committed to the deadline of 1 October for the invasion. Hitler returned to Berlin, which, it had been agreed, was were he could be most easily seized by Witzleben's troops. But they wavered at the last minute – and it was at the last minute that Neville Chamberlain came back on stage and the one-act tragedy of Munich was played out. No war would be necessary after all. The Czechs must hand over the Sudetenland to the Reich. The world sighed with relief. To arrest the Führer now, at this new pinnacle of success, would have been unthinkable. And the plotters alternated between secret relief at having the matter settled for them, and having the nerve to put the blame on Chamberlain for wrecking their plans.

The reason why Munich was one of Hitler's greatest triumphs was not only because of the skill with which he pressurized Chamberlain and Daladier – the 'little worms', as he referred to them a few months later. Nor was it a triumph because of the way in which he managed to involve both Poland (the next sacrificial victim on his list) and Hungary as partners in crime. It is an undeniable fact that his peaceful acquisition of the Czech Sudetenland was a strategic masterpiece. Seldom in history has an aggressor been able to render a prospective victim helpless with the active cooperation of his erstwhile opponents. For every one of Czechoslovakia's key defences was sited in the Sudetenland – and with those defences in his possession, Hitler could march straight into Prague any day he chose.

And that was precisely what happened on 15 March 1939 – the 'Rape of Prague'. Summoned peremptorily to Berlin before the crack of dawn, poor old Dr Emil Hácha, Czechoslovakia's President, was told that the Wehrmacht was under orders to pulverize his country in under five hours. Hácha was then pushed and shoved to the point of physical collapse by Göring and Ribbentrop until in desperation he signed a phoney appeal for the Czech provinces of Bohemia and Moravia to be taken under the protection of the Reich. This sordid scene followed weeks of careful manoeuvering aimed at getting the Slovaks to secede from Czechoslovakia, then at panicking them into submission by allowing – by encouraging – Hungary to bite off Sub-Carpathian Ruthenia from the fledgling state. On 15 March Czechoslovakia vanished from the map of Europe as an independent state – another diplomatic and strategic triumph for the Führer, with more than enough military loot to keep the generals happy. The Germans took over sufficient Czech tanks to fit out three completely new Panzer divisions – a formidable overnight addition to the strength of the German Army.

Munich, however, had been the crucial point, and it was not until after Munich, when the Germans were able to examine the former Czech defences for themselves, that it was really understood how terrifyingly close to the wind Hitler had sailed. Erich von Manstein, soon to emerge as one of the most gifted strategists and tacticians in German military history, had this to say at Nuremberg after the war about the Munich crisis. 'Neither our western border nor our Polish frontier could really have been effectively defended by us,' he testified, 'and there is no doubt whatsoever that had Czechoslovakia defended herself, we would have been held up by her fortifications, for we did not have the means to break through.' Even Hitler, after an inspection tour of the Czech 'Maginot Line', was sobered enough to comment : 'I now understand why my generals urged restraint.' But the Anglo-French sell-out at Munich, unbelievably favourable to Germany, rendered the generals' urging of restraint null and void. Any momentary qualms Hitler felt over the risks he had run before Munich were drowned in renewed floods of megalomania and false confidence in the 'little worms' swallowing a move against Poland, too.

But after the Prague coup of 15 March the 'little worms' turned – something Hitler never accepted, despite accurate reports from German officials in France and Britain. 'Hitler's broken his word,' was England's damning verdict on Prague, and *'Il faut en finir'* ('This must be stopped') began to be heard in France. After the Prague coup the Nazi propaganda orchestra began to tune up with familiar-sounding accusations of Polish atrocities against racial Germans living in Danzig and other Polish territory. But the diplomatic atmosphere began to crackle again with France and Britain issuing guarantees of military aid to Poland in the event of armed aggression from Germany.

On 22 May 1939 Hitler made the first serious blunder which would lead him to defeat in the Second World War : the signing of the 'Pact of Steel', a military alliance between the Third Reich and Mussolini's Italy. It was a blunder because in 1939 Italy was a thorough liability as a military ally. The country had no reserve stocks of war material ; fuel stocks were low and the arms and equipment of the Italian Army were obsolescent. The Italian Navy was a different story : it had a powerful, modernized battle fleet and an impressive number of fleet submarines. But the possibility of war in the immediate future was horrifying to Mussolini. Pathetically – almost as pathetically as Chamberlain and Daladier had tried 'appeasement' on Hitler – Mussolini held out for a policy of Italian 'non-belligerence', and stuck to it until he thought that he had a sufficiently enfeebled victim in France in June 1940.

Every effort Germany was subsequently forced to make to redress the mistakes and defeats of Mussolini would be debilitating and favourable to the Allies. It is one of the strangest facets of Hitler's character, this loyalty to Mussolini for the Duce's support during the *Anschluss* and the Sudeten crisis. And this from the man who six years before had commented to Hermann Rauschning, top Nazi in Danzig : 'I am willing to sign anything. I will do anything to facilitate the success of my policy . . . . There has never been a sworn treaty which has not sooner or later been broken or become untenable . . . . Why should I not make an agreement in good faith today and un-hesitatingly break it tomorrow if the future of the German people demands it ?'

Of all the Wehrmacht commanders only Grand-Admiral Raeder was pleased with the idea of being able to work with his Italian opposite numbers. The Army reports about the fighting value of the Italian Army were uncompromisingly pessimistic. Here certainly was a warning which Hitler should have taken seriously. He was to discover the immediate weakness of his Italian ally far more rapidly than the long-term strength of his enemies.

Hitler's opinion of the validity of treaties was immediately proved to be only too genuine. The Pact of Steel was signed on 22 May and it specifically stated that a period of peace of at least three years was the ideal of both Germany and Italy. But within twenty-four hours, in Berlin, Hitler was telling the Wehrmacht Commanders-in-Chief that he was in fact resolved on war in 1939. Pretext: Danzig and anti-German 'incidents' in Poland. Objective: the destruction of Poland as an independent state. The possibility of war with Britain and France: acceptable. The chance of another bloodless victory: unlikely – and irrelevant. War it must be – and this time not a word was said by the generals. Since 7 May an Army planning staff had been at work on *Fall Weiss* ('Case White') – the military destruction of Poland.

Hitler's harangue of 23 May 1939 is the clearest proof of how completely the generals had been brought to heel. In the First World War Germany had been trapped into fighting a two-front war, and ever since 1918 this had been held up by German military theorists as a disastrous mistake, never again to be repeated. Now Hitler was proposing to repeat the experiment if necessary, and the only comforter was his assurance that it would not, in all probability, be necessary. Poland could be isolated, and the 'little worms' of Munich governing France and Britain would not intervene.

It was over the isolation of Poland that Hitler scored one of the most astonishing successes of his entire career: the suborning of Soviet Russia. It was obvious that an *entente* between Britain, France, Poland and Russia could destroy Germany. The Kremlin urgently sought such an alliance, but from the start negotiations were blocked by Poland's refusal to countenance operations by Red Army forces on Polish soil, should German aggression make this necessary. Asinine diplomacy by the British and French, lacking all sense of tact or urgency, caused Stalin's patience to run out. And the result was one of the greatest diplomatic revolutions in European history: the signing of the German-Soviet Non-Aggression Pact in Moscow on 23 August 1939.

Hitler had cut it pretty fine – the date he had set for the invasion of Poland was only three days away, on 26 August – but now the problem of taking on Poland appeared in a totally different light. The Russians had agreed to give Germany a free hand. But the German attack did not go in on 26 August. On 25 August Hitler got two extremely unpleasant shocks. The first was a pathetic admission by Mussolini that Italy was totally unready for war, backed by an appalling list of raw materials and war supplies needed to put the Italian war machine on anything like a war footing. The second was the signing of a mutual assistance pact between Britain and Poland. For the first time, Hitler wavered. He called off the invasion of Poland, despite the fact that the bulk of his forces were already either on the frontier or moving up to it for the attack at dawn on the twenty-sixth. 'Stop everything at once,' he told Keitel. 'Get Brauchitsch immediately. I need time for negotiations.' Göring asked if the decision was permanent or not. 'No,' replied Hitler, 'I will have to see whether we can eliminate British intervention.'

During the next six days Hitler and Ribbentrop used every trick in the book to do so. They failed. And Hitler was now coming under pressure from the generals, who were unhappy about the possibility about having to fight a Polish campaign in the autumnal mud. Hitler did not stage-manage another Munich, but he still expected to get away with his war. He was soon undeceived by the French and British ultimatums which resulted in those two countries declaring war on Germany on 3 September; and on that same day a top-secret telegram went off to Moscow inviting Stalin to join in the Polish campaign, sending the Red Army into eastern Poland, which had already been designated a Soviet 'zone of influence' in a secret protocol tacked onto the Non-Aggression Pact.

So it was that Hitler's Wehrmacht went to war. Its commanders did not know it, but that first campaign against Poland would be the easiest they would ever have to fight.

Part II
VICTORY

POLAND: THE BLUEPRINT BLITZKRIEG

The runaway success of the Wehrmacht in Poland has usually been hailed as a model of flawless strategic planning and technical expertise, with all arms working together in perfect harmony and every man, from general to private, knowing exactly what he had to do. This, however, does not bear a detailed scrutiny. A lot went wrong on the German side during the Polish campaign, and this is not surprising. The technique of armoured warfare supported by pin-point bombing had never been tried before on a large scale (despite the much-vaunted experiments made in the Spanish Civil War) and nobody really knew how to make it work. Only the experience of battle could provide this knowledge, and it took some time before the armoured, mechanized, infantry, and air forces got into the swing of it.

This is too often forgotten. Everyone knows about the gallant Polish cavalry pitting lance and sabre against the Panzers. But how many people know about the German commander of the 2nd Motorized Division, who came into contact with Polish cavalry on the first day of the campaign and promptly asked for permission to withdraw?

In Poland the German war machine was trying out a lot of new techniques for the first time, and it made several mistakes. But from the start it made the maximum use of its advantages and won its campaign in record time. And these advantages were formidable. Never again did the Wehrmacht start a campaign with so many of them.

The first German advantage was geographical. Hitler's reduction of Czechoslovakia, plus the detachment of East Prussia from the Reich twenty-odd years before, enabled the Wehrmacht to strike at Poland in eight different directions : east and south-east from Pomerania; south-west, south, and south-east from East Prussia ; north-east from Silesia ; north and north-east from Slovakia. And all these directions added up to converging lines of advance.

The second German advantage lay in the strategy adopted by the Poles. Marshal Rydz-Smigly, the Polish C-in-C, had turned down the warning of the French who had advised him, considering the geographical weakness of the western frontier, to concentrate his forces along the Vistula river and beat the Germans there. But Rydz-Smigly was determined to fight for the 'Danzig Corridor' and the industrial and agricultural regions west of the Vistula. And 'into these Polish dispositions,' as Major-General von Mellenthin has commented, 'the German plan fitted like a glove.'

The other German advantages may be lumped together. The German Army was fully mobilized and in position, ready for the fray ; the Polish Army was not. The Wehrmacht had a modern, well-equipped air force ; the Poles did not. The German Army not only had more tanks but had concentrated them into irresistible striking forces. Far more important than the German superiority in *materiel*, however, was the fact that the French (the British did not have so much as a brigade in position by the end of the crucial phase of the campaign) had no intention whatsoever of fighting an offensive campaign in the West. Poland had to tackle the Germans without her Allies lifting a finger to help her – and with Soviet Russia poised to move in as soon as the upper hand was gained by the Germans.

Who were the key generals in the German line-up ?

The offensive was entrusted to two army groups : one operating from Pomerania/East Prussia and the other from Silesia/Slovakia. The northern group (Army Group 'B') was commanded by Colonel-General Fedor von Bock, a hatchet-faced professional who knew his trade thoroughly and kept his counsel on political matters. Bock had two armies under him : 3rd Army (General Georg von Küchler) in East Prussia and 4th Army (General Günther Hans von Kluge) in Pomerania. The most important unit in Kluge's army was General Heinz Guderian's XIX Corps, which had one Panzer division and two motorized divisions.

In the south was Army Group 'A', commanded by Colonel-General Gerd von Rundstedt. Rundstedt was, like Bock, a hard-bitten professional, òne of Germany's top-ranking generals in seniority. Rundstedt had been restored to harness after his dismissal in the shake-up after Hitler's removal of Blomberg and Fritsch in 1938. He had three armies. On the left was General Johannes Blaskowitz with 8th Army. In the centre was General Walther von Reichenau (the most enthusiastic pro-Nazi of all the German generals) with 10th Army. Down in Moravia and Slovakia was General Siegmund Wilhelm List with 14th Army, which included a mountain division to cope with the crossing of the Carpathians.

Both army groups were backed by a *Luftflotte* – an air fleet. General Albert Kesselring's *Luftflotte* I was attached to Army Group 'B' ; General Alexander Löhr's *Luftflotte* IV to Army Group 'A'. Between them the two *Luftflotten* had an air striking force of 897 bombers and 297 Stuka dive-bombers, the latter of which proved themselves adept at pin-point attacks on bridges, railway centres and troop concentrations.

The German strategy practised in the Polish campaign has been summed up in a much-quoted but descriptive blanket phrase : 'the inner and outer pincers', whose bite converted the central drive on Warsaw by 8th and 10th Armies into a battle of destruction. The closing of the 'inner pincers' pierced the 'Danzig Corridor', put Warsaw under siege, and surrounded all Polish forces west of the Vistula. The 'outer pincers', meeting south of Brest Litovsk, made the defeat of the Polish armies a total one and achieved the long-cherished dream of a *Schlacht ohne Morgen :* a battle without a morrow.

Star performer in the first phase – the fight for the Corridor –

was Guderian with XIX Corps. The first corps commander ever to direct a battle from the front in wireless-equipped command vehicles, Guderian had smashed the Polish army defending the Corridor by 4 September. By 6 September he was across the Vistula, having impressed the visiting Hitler the previous day with what Panzer forces could do by showing him the debris of a smashed artillery regiment. On 8 September Guderian's XIX Corps was ordered to move to East Prussia and spearhead the advance of Küchler's 3rd Army in the direction of Brest Litovsk.

On the same day Rundstedt's north-easterly drive against Warsaw was halted. A rapid advance by Reichenau's 10th Army was checked by fierce resistance before the capital. The hard-fought siege of Warsaw began, with the surrounded Polish armies west of the Vistula falling back to the east in a ponderous attempt to break through the German ring and join hands with the Warsaw garrison. This brought about the biggest crisis of the campaign for the Germans. Between 10 September and 13 September the 'Battle of the Bzura' was fought, when the Polish 'Poznan' and 'Pomorze' Armies surged across the Bzura river and took the German 8th Army in flank. The day was saved by prompt action on the part of Rundstedt, who swung Reichenau's 10th Army to the north to support 8th Army while Stukas concentrated on the Polish bridgeheads across the Bzura. Forced back across the Bzura, the Polish masses recoiled on Kutno where they finally surrendered on 19 September.

With the surrender of the 170,000 Poles in the Kutno pocket on 19 September, the Polish campaign was virtually over. On 15 September Guderian had closed in on Brest Litovsk and had pushed 3rd Panzer Division even further to the south. On 17 September, 3rd Panzer made contact with the advance spearheads of Army Group 'A' at Wlodawa on the River Bug; and on the same day the Red Army rolled into eastern Poland. This dashed all Polish hopes of a last stand in the east. The rest of the campaign was one long mopping-up operation, with Warsaw itself holding out gallantly until surrendering to Blaskowitz's 8th Army on 28 September. This was six days after the

Germans and Russians had met at Brest Litovsk, the Germans pulling back to their side of the prearranged demarcation-line.

Both of the German army group commanders came out of the Polish campaign well: Bock for the speed at which he had switched Guderian's armoured corps from the Corridor to East Prussia for the decisive drive on Brest Litovsk ; Rundstedt for his decisive handling of the crisis on the Bzura. Kluge and Reichenau emerged as the 'top-scoring' army commanders, and Guderian, by virtue of his remarkable performance throughout the whole campaign, as the most prominent corps commander of mobile forces. But despite the incredible speed with which the whole campaign had been brought to its successful con-clusion, the victorious generals were requited in a singularly cool manner. And not without reason.

The German Army learned two main lessons from the Polish campaign. The first was the value of speed, of penetration in depth with the Panzers to the fore. Bypass resistance, drive on into the enemy's rear, leave strongpoints and heavy troop concentrations to the infantry – that was the essence of *Blitzkrieg*, which really boiled down to preventing the enemy from being able to retreat and fight again. The second lesson, following naturally from the first, was the value of close cooperation between the ground forces and the precision bomber crews of the Luftwaffe. The bombers learned to go for the key targets behind the enemy's front, break up his reserves, disrupt his communications. At the same time the Luftwaffe had the immediate tactical job of coping with obstacles in the path of the advancing Panzers.

But the Wehrmacht commanders also found that much had still to be resolved. Apart from far-sighted leaders like Guderian (who was still a comparatively junior general) very few of the generals of the German Army had grasped that the Panzers must be allowed to set their own pace and must not be shackled to that of the infantry columns plodding in their wake. It was natural that the infantry commanders should feel that they were being left to do all the fighting while the Panzers dashed onward into the blue. It was also natural that army commanders (Kluge was a case in point) should try to prevent their Panzer generals from cutting loose on their own. Conversely, heralds of the new armoured warfare, such as Guderian, complained that excessive subordination to army control tied them down and wasted invaluable opportunities. But the problem was not settled after the Polish campaign ; it was not settled before the great battles of 1940, and it was not even settled when the Wehrmacht invaded Russia in June 1941.

A more sophisticated partnership between the Panzers and the infantry was the prime need, and it could only come into being as a result of a firm directive from above. And one thing was abundantly clear after the Polish campaign : the channels of command were not what they should be. Were the field commanders of the Army really required to take the frequent counter-orders from Hitler's HQ – or was the official Army High Command merely a rubber stamp?

Who, in fact, was running the Army in the field – the General Staff, or Hitler ?

AFTER POLAND: THE
GENERALS KEPT AT HEEL

On 1 September, the first day of the war, Hitler had inflicted an unusually pompous proclamation on the German Army in which he stated : 'I am from now on just the first soldier of the German Reich. I have once more put on that coat that was most sacred and dear to me. I will not take it off again until victory is assured, or I will not survive the outcome.' Bombastic though it was, this was in fact one of the promises which Hitler actually kept. And he wasted no time in making it clear to his generals that he was, in word and deed, 'the first soldier of the Reich'.

Napoleon had laid down that the ideal constitution should be short and obscure, and Hitler had certainly taken pains to make as few definitions as possible as to who would really be giving the orders when the shooting started. The chain of command established after the weeding-out of Blomberg and Fritsch in February 1938 was heavy and lopsided, but built into it was a manual over-riding device which Hitler never let out of his own hand. He himself, as Supreme Commander of the German Armed Forces, studied the situation reports and appropriate orders sent to Armed Forces High Command by the staffs of the Army, Navy and Air Force high commands (OKH for the Army, OKM for the Navy, and OKL for the

Luftwaffe). Then, via Keitel and Jodl, Hitler would issue his own orders for relaying down the line to the three services.

In theory, Hitler's orders should have been little more than a rubber-stamp confirmation of the decisions already made by his professional generals and admirals. But, as we have already seen, Hitler had always had a deep-seated contempt for the military professionals. In those incredible four years between the tearing-up of the Versailles Treaty in 1935 and the peaceful destruction of Czechoslovakia in 1938-39, Hitler had proved time and again that the generals' opinion was not worth a button. This alone made it inevitable that he would be breathing down their necks when they told him that such-and-such was the key objective, to be secured inside such-and-such a time limit. But there was far more to it than that.

One of Hitler's most frightening characteristics was his mastery of detail. Unlike the absurd, half-baked *obiter dicta* he loved to make on the subject of world historical forces, he had a photographic memory when it came to the hard facts of military hardware. At times he appeared to be a walking encyclopedia of the battle-worthiness of every unit in the German Army, reeling off figures on how many shells 10th Division had in its ammunition-dumps and how many more were on the way; how effective a new type of field gun was proving in comparison with older weapons ; how tank crews were getting on with a heavier turret gun, etc. Hitler could keep this up for hours and he found it one of his best weapons in deflating his so-called military 'experts'. A general, asked by Hitler out of the blue how much petrol his army or corps had for the next forty-eight hours would almost certainly have to apologize and say that he would have to consult his staff. That general would then have to swallow the embarrassment and humiliation of being told the state of his petrol stocks by the Führer himself – as likely as not with Keitel smirking obsequiously in the background. The effect of this trick can be imagined. Useless to point out that these details were not a general's concern, that that was what his staff was for! It was a devastating way of undermining a professional soldier's confidence in himself, and Hitler used it without mercy.

It should be noted, in passing, that Hitler's grasp of detail was entirely focussed on the German Army. This can be said to have been one of the biggest strokes of fortune for the Allies in the Second World War. The mind boggles at what might have happened if Hitler had bullied Göring into building fleets of long-range, four-engined bombers, or if he had mastered the techniques of U-boat construction and submarine warfare and given Dönitz his head. But the Army remained his prime concern. It was the misfortune of the Army and its commanders that Hitler had not been a stoker in the Imperial Navy, or an air gunner (or even mechanic) in the Imperial Army Flying Corps. He had been a soldier, and he was out to prove himself in high command. Hitler might almost have said, as did Winston Churchill when recalling his impressions on becoming Prime Minister in 1940 : 'I thought I knew a great deal about it all, and I was sure I would not fail.'

When it came to Hitler proving how much he knew about it all, the man who came off worst was General Franz Ritter von Halder, Army Chief-of-Staff and popularly believed to be the best brain in the Army. Halder was the man who refined the details of the campaign for submission to the Führer ; and Halder had to swallow the constant mortification of having his plans altered because they were not bold enough, or because they were concentrating on an inferior objective, or because Hitler felt that they were simply wrong. Halder could state, with complete justification, that it had been Hitler's order to switch the main thrust east of Warsaw that led to the crisis on the Bzura. It had – but in the overview it had also spelled the total defeat of the Polish armies.

Halder, therefore, was the general who came out of the Polish campaign with the biggest sense of grievance that he was not being allowed to do his job properly. But there was a much wider sense of grievance. The generals as a whole, from army down to division, felt that their achievements had been unfairly played down – like a winning football team grousing because the manager has claimed all the credit. And the outcome was another feeble attempt by the generals to re-assert themselves, an attempt which Hitler strangled at birth.

The most immediate cause of this new ripple of discontent among the generals was not merely injured vanity, however. Hitler, after discovering that Britain and France were only too ready to reject the overtures for peace which he made after the fall of Poland, suddenly began to demand an immediate assault on Belgium, Holland and France for November 1939. His reason was that time was working against Germany and that the French and British armies must be flattened with a quick knock-out blow before they got too strong. As a practical proposition, however, this was out of the question. Not only did the German Army have to be redeployed : its mobile forces needed re-equipping. Worse still, ammunition stocks were low – far too low for an immediate campaign in the West.

On 10 October Hitler called a meeting of the Army commanders and served them with *Führer Directive For the Conduct of the War No. 6 :* a lengthy memorandum on how the campaign in the West was to be fought. The reaction was unanimous : the thing could not be done as early as Hitler wanted. One general, however, went further and raised a moral objection. He was Colonel-General Wilhelm Ritter von Leeb, commander of Army Group 'C' in the Siegfried Line and responsible for the defence of Germany's western frontier. On 11 October Leeb wrote a memorandum pointing out that deep moral opprobrium would attach to Germany if neutral Belgium were to be attacked for the second time within twenty-five years. Leeb's memorandum was additional ammunition for Brauchitsch when he went back to Hitler on 17 October and tried to talk the Führer out of the attack in the West. Needless to say, Brauchitsch got nowhere. And ten days later the situation came to a head. At the New Chancellery in Berlin Hitler awarded the Knight's Cross of the Iron Cross to twenty-four generals (Guderian among them) and went on to give Brauchitsch and Halder a deadline for the assault on the West : 12 November.

This sparked off another twitching of conspiracy to remove Hitler, which proved to be a depressing replica of its predecessor at the time of Munich. Halder, Beck, Goerdeler, and the others all agreed that Hitler must be removed if he went ahead with an attack in the West. Now, however, Halder was expressing reservations about the ethics of staging a coup while Germany's enemies were still in the field. Brauchitsch shilly-shallied as usual : if anyone was going to take a firm lead in deposing Hitler, it was not going to be the Army. After a week of whispering, however, the conspiracy was effectively torpedoed by Hitler himself.

He chose his moment well. Brauchitsch had finally worked up sufficient nerve to ask for an audience in which he proposed to read Hitler a lengthy document arguing against the Western campaign. He got his audience on 5 November (the day scheduled for the first movement of troops to their final jumping-off stations) – but it was not a private audience. Brauchitsch did not get the chance to read his memorandum as intended. Instead he started by asking for the Führer's guarantee that OKH, the Army High Command, would be granted sole responsibility for the conduct of future campaigns. Brauchitsch then came out with the incredible and totally untrue statement that troop morale was bad and that defeatism was rife. Hitler promptly counter-attacked with a torrent of sarcastic abuse, of which the sum total was that the Army generals did not want to fight. Brauchitsch, thoroughly cowed, went back to Army Supreme HQ at Zossen in a state approaching nervous collapse – and the conspiracy fizzled out.

Nevertheless, Hitler did postpone the Western offensive on 7 November. On 9 November he postponed it again. In all there were to be fourteen postponements, for which many explanations have been offered : repeatedly bad weather, uneasiness at how much information had leaked out, the need to build up ammunition stocks – even a common-sense revulsion against the thought of a winter campaign. But one reason stands out above all the rest : Hitler was not happy with the basic plan.

He was right. Champions of Hitler's brilliance have to admit that, whatever the original Army plan – *Fall Gelb* ('Case Yellow') – boasted in the way of detailed thought, it was never-the-less nothing more than a scaled-up rehash of the notorious 'Schlieffen Plan' followed in 1914. This had provided for holding actions on the German left and a massive, scything wheel through the Low Countries on the right, eventually driving between Paris and the French coast. There were, of course, many differences between 1914 and 1939. In the age of the aeroplane it was certainly vital that the airfields and ports of the Channel Coast must be snatched from the Allies and turned against them. Nevertheless, it was obvious to the meanest intelligence that the Allies would move into Belgium to meet such an advance head-on. What guarantees were there that deadlock and its inevitable sequence, trench warfare, would not ensue ?

Hitler never got a sensible reply out of Brauchitsch and Halder on this point. Naturally. As long as the arguing went on over details – let alone over such fundamental points as this – the offensive in the West must be postponed, and nothing suited their book better. Unknown to Hitler, however, a hidden ally was working on similar lines to his own. This was General Erich von Manstein, Chief-of-Staff to Rundstedt, who would lead the central army group in the attack on the West. Manstein argued that it would be pointless merely to push the Allies back to the line of the Somme – the furthest territorial advance that he thought possible. Such a leaden collision would not and could not result in a battle of annihilation. Manstein's project stood the original Schlieffen Plan on its head. It envisaged a sufficiently strong advance on the German right to get the Allies to charge forward into Belgium in order to block it. A concentrated breakthrough launched from the German centre – through the Ardennes – could then slice westward towards the Channel and catch the Allies in Belgium in a gigantic trap.

With the approval of his chief, Rundstedt, Manstein drew up his plan in memorandum form and sent it up to OKH. He did this not once but five times : on 31 October, on 21 November, on 30 November, on 6 December, and on 18 December. Each time, however, Manstein's memoranda were sat on by Brauchitsch and Halder and never got through to OKW. As the last days of 1939 approached, *Fall Gelb* still stood as the basic plan, although it was clocking up a record number of postponements. But Hitler was still not convinced that it was a genuinely watertight plan.

He made no bones about concealing his discontent with his professional generals. Guderian recalls that between the investiture on 27 October and 23 November the generals were subjected to a course of lectures in Berlin, conducted among others by Goebbels, Göring, and finally Hitler. In these lectures no punches were pulled. It was made clear to the generals that the regime felt that complete trust could not be put in the commanders of the Army. This caused the deepest offence. Guderian's account goes on to state how he conferred with Manstein and Rundstedt, neither of whom were prepared to protest. Guderian went on to Reichenau, to whom the generals looked as a pro-Nazi and therefore closest to Hitler's favour. Reichenau told him that he and Hitler were not on good terms, and Guderian thereupon took the extremely bold step of requesting a face-to-face interview himself. He got his interview – a sobering one. Hitler admitted 'It's a question of the Commander-in-Chief of the Army', but refused to admit that he must either learn to trust Brauchitsch or sack him. Nor did any other name come up in the conversation which Hitler found acceptable. Guderian came empty away from his hour's interview, in his own words 'deeply depressed by the insight that I had gained'.

So matters stood in the first days of 1940. Hitler was not going to restore full tactical command to the Army High Command. In snapping the generals back on their leash he had generated deep distrust and had admitted that it was mutual. Come what may, he would go ahead with his assault in the West, although the final plans for the assault had yet to be defined.

But not for long.

SHARPENING THE SICKLE

Great minds, we are told, think alike, and nothing is more fascinating than to trace the way in which the ideas of Hitler and those of Manstein eventually merged. Hitler's underlying dissatisfaction with *Fall Gelb* warred with his instinct to fall upon the French and British at the earliest opportunity. As early as 9 November he had stated that the armoured strength of Army Group 'A' (Rundstedt) needed raising. On 20 November he went further, ordering OKH to work out plans for shifting the main weight of the offensive to the Ardennes sector if the going should prove easier there than on Bock's front in Belgium and Holland. But on 10 January 1940 an accident occurred which spelled death to *Fall Gelb*. A liaison aircraft crashed behind the Belgian lines with a full set of the *Gelb* plans abroad. These plans were not totally destroyed (despite frantic efforts by their bearer, Luftwaffe Major Reinberger, to burn them) and it had to be assumed that the basic details of *Gelb* were now known to the Allies.

The next major conference, on what must be done to modify *Gelb*, was held on 20 January. Little emerged in the way of practicalities, although Hitler once more raised the possibility of launching a major attack south of Liege. Meanwhile, on 12 January, Manstein had fired off another of his memoranda into the obstructive sandbag of OKH, which met with the fate of its predecessors. But on 30 January Hitler's personal aide, Colonel Rudolf Schmundt, paid a visit to Rundstedt and Manstein at Koblenz during a tour of the front – and he returned to Hitler with the electrifying news that Army Group 'A' had evolved a detailed plan which was a refinement of the Führer's own ideas.

Schmundt's visit came just in time, for Manstein was already under notice to quit Rundstedt's HQ and take up a corps command. He left Koblenz on 8 February, but Hitler interviewed him on 17 February and from then on events moved fast. Brauchitsch and Halder were summoned to the presence on the eighteenth and watched Hitler take a map and draw in the new line of advance envisaged by Manstein. And on the twenty-fourth the new plan was signed and sealed. Rundstedt, not Bock, would carry the main offensive now, and an entirely new unit would act as its spearhead. This was the *Panzergruppe*, of seven Panzer divisions and three motorized divisions. The *Panzergruppe* – the biggest concentration of mechanized and armoured forces yet used by the German Army – was entrusted to General Ewald von Kleist, by no means a Panzer virtuoso but held in high regard at OKH. This campaign would be Kleist's first real experience in working with Panzer forces, but he was not alone. One of the Panzer divisions which would come under his command – a new division, the 7th, formed since the Polish campaign – had been handed over on 15 February to a general untried in Panzer tactics whose name was soon to become legend : Erwin Rommel.

In the First World War the young Rommel had won the *Pour le Mérite* for conspicuous successes as an infantry officer, particularly in mountain warfare. Soldiering on with the *Reichswehr* after the Treaty of Versailles, Rommel had come to Hitler's attention by writing and publishing a handbook on infantry tactics – *Infanterie Greift An* – in the 1930s. As a colonel he was given the job of supervising the military training of the *Hitler Jugend* – but that did not last long. Rommel soon clashed with the *Hitler Jugend*'s arrogant boss Baldur von Schirach, and returned to Army duty at the Wiener Neustadt War Academy. Then, in October 1938, Rommel was personally selected by Hitler to command the *Führergleitbataillon* – the Führer's bodyguard. It was in this rôle that Rommel followed the Polish campaign, but he was the complete opposite of a staff officer, let alone of a courtier. He not only asked for an active command ; he asked for a Panzer command. And he got 7th Panzer Division, which was destined to put up one of the most remarkable performances in the coming campaign in the West.

So it was that *Gelb* was transformed into *Sichelschnitt* – the sweep of the sickle. But as February gave place to March, and the war games and conferences continued to explore all the problems and possibilities that lay ahead, all was by no means settled. The commanders of Bock's Army Group 'B' were worried that too much of their former strength had been carved off and handed over to Rundstedt. The main axis of advance of the *Panzergruppe* – assuming, many thought, that it ever did manage to get through the Ardennes and cross the Meuse near Sedan – had not been agreed. But, as from 26 February 1940, all these worries became secondary. Out of the blue had come a directive for a new campaign, a total distraction from what had always been pressed upon the Army as the 'decisive battle' which would end the war.

Denmark and Norway were to be conquered before a shot was fired in the West.

NORWAY: THE NAVY STEALS THE LIMELIGHT

The German northern offensive of April-May 1940 was unique. It ranks as one of the most successful coups ever achieved by Hitler's Wehrmacht: a lightning land attack delivered to its destination by sea power and carried through to its triumphant conclusion under the shield of air supremacy. Such a summing-up, however, implies that long and careful planning, with the closest cooperation between the land, sea, and air high commands earned its just reward. But nothing is further from the truth.

The Norwegian campaign was planned completely off the cuff. The Army and the Luftwaffe were kept right out of the discussions until absolutely necessary – and this when the next agreed move was the *Sichelschnitt* offensive in the West. The service which would get the most benefit out of Norway was the Navy and there were plenty of sound strategic reasons why Norway should be taken. But for sheer muddle and confusion and snap decisions, the evolution of the Norwegian campaign is hard to beat.

To start with, Hitler had wanted to keep Norway neutral. The reason was simple. Germany's annual consumption of iron ore was fifteen million tons, and with the establishment of the Allied blockade on the outbreak of war in 1939 it was vital that Germany should continue to import at least eleven million tons

from Sweden. The main outlet for the Swedish ore was through
the Norwegian port of Narvik, and from Narvik German
freighters could steam right to the doorstep of the Reich under
protection of Norwegian territorial waters, where Allied
cruisers could not get at them. But when Soviet Russia attacked
Finland on 30 November 1939 it was obvious that the Germans
would not be able to get away with this for much longer.

For the Finns held out, to the relief and applause of the free
world, and the British and French agreed to prepare a joint
expeditionary force to send to Finland's aid. But this could
only be done through Narvik, with the connivance of Norway
and Sweden, and it would be the easiest thing in the world for
the Allies to cut off the German shipments of ore once established at Narvik. So it was that Hitler began to listen to Grand-
Admiral Raeder's arguments for German landings in Norway
to forestall this threat.

Raeder had always believed that the Kaiser's Germany had
made a vital mistake in the First World War. By neglecting to
conquer Norway, Germany was forced to rely on the naval
bases of the homeland and submit to the British blockade,
which was clamped across the northern exit of the North Sea
like a manhole cover. This mistake meant that the Imperial
German High Seas Fleet never lived up to its title, but was
forced to restrict itself to operations in the North Sea. German
naval bases in Norway would enable the Reich to turn the
North Sea blockade and unleash submarine and surface raiders
against Britain's Atlantic supply-lines. And Raeder started by
backing the wildly-exaggerated claims of the Norwegian traitor,
Vidkun Quisling, that a sizeable majority of Norwegians could
be found to back a German takeover of Norway in the name of
national security.

Hitler did not interview Quisling until 14 December, when
the Russo-Finnish war had been in progress for a fortnight.
It was not exactly a timely moment for the Navy to be advocat-
ing a seaborne operation, for the first news of *Graf Spee*'s
depressing performance in the Battle of the River Plate had
started to come in. Not that the Naval Staff was at all
enthusiastic about the proposition of taking on Norway:

Raeder's advisers concluded that Allied intervention in Norway was unlikely, that for Germany to move in would be a dangerous undertaking', and that the status quo should be maintained as long as possible. But this was just what the Russo-Finnish war had made impossible, and Hitler was extremely dissatisfied. On 27 January he ordered Keitel and Jodl to continue with outline plans for Norway under the code-name *Weserübung* – 'Exercise Weser'.

This was three days before Schmundt visited Koblenz and found out about Manstein's *Sichelschnitt* plan. And in mid-February Hitler's subsequent consultations with Manstein coincided with the event which precipitated the Norwegian campaign. This was Britain's seizure of the German supply-ship *Altmark* in Norwegian territorial waters on 17 February. It was not merely a public announcement that no one was going to run British prisoners (*Altmark* had been carrying merchant seamen POWs from victims of the *Graf Spee*) through neutral waters. It convinced Hitler that Norway could do nothing to prevent the British doing as they liked in Norwegian territorial waters ; and he immediately decided, quite rightly, to get his blow in first.

On 17 February Hitler had been discussing *Sichelschnitt* with Manstein. On 19 February he ordered Keitel and Jodl to rush forward *Weserübung*. Jodl pointed out that an Army C-in-C must be selected and Keitel came up with the name of General Nikolaus von Falkenhorst, commanding a corps in the West, who happened to have fought in Finland in 1918. And on 21 February a very surprised Falkenhorst was summoned to Berlin. What he heard from Hitler surprised him even more.

It started, for Falkenhorst, with a detailed interrogation on his experiences during the Finnish campaign of 1918. Hitler then took him over to a map table, told him that the British were up to no good in Scandinavia, and gave him five hours in which to go away, draw up a plan for forestalling the British, and report back. This was, basically, an extremely unorthodox *viva voce* initiative test. Falkenhorst was told that he would be given five divisions for the job – but that was all the briefing he got. He was not told anything about the preliminary spade-work put in by the OKW planners. Nothing more : objective Norway, five divisions, deadline for solution five hours. Falkenhorst's most pressing problem, however, was the fact that he knew absolutely nothing about Norway. But he reacted in a direct – if somewhat unmilitary – fashion : 'I went out and bought a Baedeker travel guide.'

Five hours later, however, he was back at the Chancellery showing Hitler his 'plan'. As Falkenhorst himself pointed out, there was very little that could be done with five divisions other than to go for the five main ports along the Norwegian coast : Oslo, Stavanger, Bergen, Trondheim, and the all-important Narvik. Hitler approved and gave Falkenhorst the go-ahead to work out the details. Now, for the very first time, Brauchitsch and Halder found out about this totally new campaign when Falkenhorst turned up at OKH on 26 February asking for spare troops, especially mountain units. The two OKH chiefs were naturally incensed, but it did them little good. Perhaps they derived some comfort from seeing Göring's rage at having been kept out of the secret when Hitler issued his formal directive for *Weserübung* on 1 March. By this time, however, the original plan had been expanded : Denmark was to be taken *en passant* : 'The crossing of the Danish border and the landings in Norway must take place simultaneously.'

The planning raced ahead. On 3 March Hitler laid it down that *Weserübung* would in fact precede *Sichelschnitt*. There was every reason for haste, for the Russians had thrown a second and much heavier offensive against the Finns, and the Finnish Army was starting to bend under the pressure. The British and French were urging Norway and Sweden to permit the transference of an Allied expeditionary force across their territory, and although these requests had been turned down there was no reason to believe that this state of affairs would endure. However, on 12 March Finland capitulated : a respite both for the Allies and for Hitler, for the Finnish surrender deprived both sides of the excuse for landing in Norway.

Yet the surrender of the Finns made little real impact on the train of events which their former resistance had set in motion. In France Daladier fell and the new premier, Paul Reynaud, was eager to take action against the 'iron route' down the Norwegian coast. In Germany Raeder pestered Hitler to make up his mind about *Weserübung*, reminding him that the winter ice in the Baltic narrows and the Norwegian Leads would soon break up. And the upshot was a head-on collision course between the rival plans. The executive order for *Weserübung* went out on 2 April, the operation being set for the ninth. The Allies finally decided to go ahead with their project for mining the waters of the 'iron route' on the eighth, holding troops in readiness to counter the inevitable German reaction.

The fact remained, however, that the German planners had won a twenty-four-hour lead over those of the Allies – and those twenty-four hours would be enough.

Falkenhorst's descent on Norway was laid squarely on the shoulders of the German Navy, and Raeder's planners had produced an extremely complex and neatly-timed schedule. Naval task forces would steam simultaneously into Narvik, Trondheim, Bergen and Oslo and land troops. Paratroops would cope with Stavanger and Oslo airfield. The Navy would land other forces at Kristiansand and Arendal – Norway's southernmost extremity. The ships would head boldly inshore and bluff their way in if possible. A battle squadron – the tough battle-cruisers *Scharnhorst* and *Gneisenau* – would distract the Royal Navy's Home Fleet. To make sure of the timing, the ships which had the most northerly passages to make would sail on 3 April. General Hans Geissler's X *Fliegerkorps* – 500 transports for airborne troops, 290 bombers, 40 Stukas, and 100 fighters – would guarantee air cover.

The assault on Denmark and Norway went in at dawn on 9 April, and it scored nine out of ten. Denmark was overrun within hours, with hardly a shot being fired. In the far north, Commodore Paul Bonte's ten destroyers landed General Eduard Dietl's mountain troops, who speedily seized the port. Trondheim also fell without a fight. At Bergen the light cruiser *Königsberg* was crippled by shellfire but the troops still went in and took the city. The paratroops had no trouble at Stavanger ; nor did the soldiers landed at Kristiansand and Arendal. Oslo, however, proved a much tougher nut to crack. The first seaborne assault, which headed in boldly straight up the fjord, was repulsed with the loss of the heavy cruiser *Blücher*, and with the pocket-battleship *Lützow* suffering heavy damage. The surviving troops were forced to land far down the fjord, and it was left to the Luftwaffe to pull the chestnuts out of the fire at Oslo, taking Fornebu airfield and holding it until the ground forces joined up.

Within twenty-four hours of the initial landings, the first stage of the plan which had started life between the covers of a Baedeker travel guide had been brilliantly accomplished. All five of the key Norwegian ports were in German hands.

But within another twenty-four hours it became clear that the Allies were not going to let the Wehrmacht get away with this latest coup. At Narvik Captain Warburton-Lee's destroyers attacked the much larger German destroyer squadron and savaged it, cutting off Dietl's mountain troops and sinking the ship carrying most of his ammunition supply as they retreated down the fjord. On 11 April Dietl's force suffered again when the *Alster*, carrying the transport for the Narvik garrison, was sunk. And on the thirteenth the British battleship *Warspite* came up the fjord with nine destroyers and wiped out the last German warships left at Narvik. Dietl and his men were on their own, beyond the reach of any immediate reinforcement – but they were saved by the caution of the Allies.

On 14 April the first Allied forces landed in Norway – but they did not attack Dietl's isolated force at Narvik, nor did they go straight for Trondheim, which the Germans must hold if they wanted to retain a hope of eventually reinforcing Dietl at Narvik. Instead the Allies landed at Andalsnes and Namsos, to the south-west and north-east of Trondheim respectively, and prepared for a pincer movement against Trondheim. It never came off. The Luftwaffe commanded the sky and kept up constant attacks on the Allied troopships and transports, and the troops that did get ashore were lacking their full equipment. A British column from Andalsnes pushed down the Gudbrandsdal valley to Lillehammer but was flung out by the German 163rd Division, racing north from Oslo, on 21 April – the first clash between British and German troops in the Second

World War. (The commander of the 163rd Division, General Erwin Engelbrecht, had had a narrow escape when the *Blücher* went down in Oslo fjord and he had to swim for it, but this mishap had no effects on the energy with which he hounded his troops northward after the fall of the capital.) On the twenty-sixth, the day that the German force operating from Trondheim was relieved by troops coming north from Oslo, the Franco-British Supreme War Council made the belated decision to evacuate central Norway and concentrate everything against Narvik. Dietl's worst ordeal was about to begin. The troubles which had beset him ever since he had landed at Narvik on the ninth were nothing to the ones in pickle for him now.

The first British troops had landed in the Narvik region on 15 April, but the reluctance with which the British Army commander grasped the nettle of a direct assault gave Dietl a respite. A tough and resourceful commander, he rounded up 2,600 survivors from the German destroyers sunk by the British, armed them with captured Norwegian weapons, and told them that they were 'mountain marine battalions'. But the fresh forces which landed north of Narvik between 28 April and 7 May outnumbered him by more than three to one. The French, British, and local Norwegian troops closed remorselessly in on Narvik over the following days. Desperate attempts were made to reinforce Dietl by air – 137th Mountain Regiment was dropped into the Narvik perimeter after a snap course of parachute training – but all to no avail. Dietl was finally forced out of Narvik on 28 May and pulled eastwards into the mountains. His position was quite hopeless. Before him lay the Allies and certain defeat ; behind him lay the Swedish frontier, surrender, and internment. Even in this sorry predicament, however, Dietl kept his head. He pulled slowly back along the iron-ore railway leading to the Swedish frontier, grudging every inch – and his tenacity was rewarded. On 7 June his patrols found to their astonishment that the Allies had pulled out.

Two tardy half-measures, at Trondheim and at Narvik, had lost the Allies the campaign. A concentrated blow at Narvik, capturing the port and forming a solid front to the south of it, would still have deprived Hitler of his Swedish iron ore and kept northern Norway free. But the earlier delays proved fatal. And on 10 May the Norwegian theatre suddenly became very unimportant indeed, for the great German offensive in the West began. To add bitterness to the Allied situation, it would soon become apparent that Andalsnes, Namsos and Narvik were only blueprints for Dunkirk.

Weserübung was the most significant contribution made by the German Navy's surface fleet in the Second World War. Without the Navy fulfilling its extremely sophisticated pattern of deadlines, surprise could never have been gained. Once ashore, the German Army commanders fulfilled their programme with gusto, particularly Engelbrecht – but it was Dietl who emerged from the campaign as the 'victor of Narvik', the fêted hero, decorated with the Knight's Cross, and with his troops awarded a special 'Narvik' commemorative badge. Master-mind Falkenhorst (for all his skill with a Baedeker) was a less glamorous character. He remained in Norway as military commander-in-chief.

Throughout the Norwegian campaign the generals at both OKW and OKH were hard put to it to stop Hitler panicking. His much-vaunted 'iron nerves' did not take kindly to the worries caused by the isolation of Dietl in Narvik and the Allied landings – at one stage he came out with the fatuous order that Dietl and his men must be evacuated by air. He continued to worry and nag Keitel, Jodl, Brauchitsch, Halder, and even Göring, until he heard that Trondheim was secure – and immediately unleashed the attack in the West.

HOLLAND AND BELGIUM: THE 'MATADOR'S CAPE'

Fedor von Bock and his deputy army commanders need not have worried so much about Rundstedt's Army Group 'A' being given the lion's share of the Panzer divisions. Army Group 'B's task was to create as much uproar as possible in Holland and Belgium, in order to get the French and British armies to lumber forward across the Franco-Belgian frontier and dutifully stick their heads in the trap. For this purpose the modern spectre of airborne and parachute forces rapidly proved a far more efficient lure than tanks. And if Army Group 'A' had got all the armour, Army Group 'B' had the cream of the Luftwaffe's tough and well-trained airborne and paratroop units.

So it was that the first German generals to hit the headlines in this first phase of the battle for the West were the Luftwaffe and Army commanders who launched the 'Trojan Horse' attacks on Holland and Belgium. Top Luftwaffe general was Albert Kesselring of *Luftflotte* II, the supporting air fleet of Army Group 'B'. In the brief Dutch campaign Kesselring's transport aircraft had the job of studding airborne and paratroop forces along a corridor connecting the Maas estuary bridge at Moerdijk, Rotterdam, and The Hague. At The Hague, General Hans Graf von Sponeck and his 22nd Infantry Division, flown in by Junkers Ju-52 transports, were under orders to occupy the three airfields around the Dutch capital – Valkenburg, Ockenburg, and Ypenburg – then move into The Hague and demand the surrender of Queen Wilhelmina's Government. Meanwhile, Luftwaffe General Kurt Student's 7th Airborne Division was to seize Rotterdam's Waalhaven airfield and the bridges in the city, together with the Moerdijk bridges.

At dawn on 10 May both these airborne attacks went in, but they met with very different fortune. Sponeck's men took their three airfields near The Hague, but were flung off them within hours by spirited counter-attacks by the alert Dutch I Corps. Sponeck himself was wounded and over 1,000 German prisoners were taken ; and although the survivors remained in the field their mission had been a resounding failure. Not so with Student and the 7th Airborne. By the evening of 10 May his men had taken Waalhaven, the Rotterdam bridges, and the Moerdijk bridges. Now they had to hang on until the ground forces could battle their way through and take over from them.

For Holland, Bock had earmarked Küchler's 18th Army, which was spearheaded by one Panzer division, the 9th. It took 9th Panzer forty-eight hours to advance from the German frontier at Gennep through s'Hertogenbosch to the Maas estuary, joining up with Student's men at Moerdijk. The road to Rotterdam and The Hague was open, and on 13 May the indomitable Queen Wilhelmina reluctantly accepted that she must leave the country as advised. Within twenty-four hours Panzer commander General Rudolf Schmidt was parleying for the surrender of Rotterdam when a crass breakdown in ground-air communications resulted in the notorious 'horror raid' on the city. The German ground signallers did everything they could to get through to Kesselring's bombers but in vain ; and the result was the razing of one of Europe's most beautiful old cities and the death of 900 citizens (a figure monstrously inflated at the time to 35,000). Accident though it was, the Rotterdam blitz had decisive results. It happened on the afternoon of 14 May, and the Dutch surrendered at 0930 hours on the following morning. Their C-in-C, General Winkelman, was determined to spare The Hague and Utrecht the fate of Rotterdam.

Küchler and Kesselring had taken a mere five days to cope with Holland, at the end of which time events were approaching the decisive stage in Belgium.

Belgium presented a much more formidable problem than Holland in the shape of the Albert Canal, a steep-sided artificial waterway which had been converted into one of the most effective-looking anti-tank ditches in western Europe. Lynchpin of the Albert Canal defences was Fort Eben-Emael in the Liege sector, reputedly one of the strongest forts in the world, with all the classic Maginot Line features such as concrete blockhouses, observation domes, pop-up gun turrets, and a troglodyte garrison. The Germans had not only to eliminate Eben-Emael: they had to seize the Albert Canal bridges before the Belgians could blow them up, to secure the passage of Reichenau's 6th Army and its two Panzer divisions, 3rd and 4th, westward towards Louvain and Brussels.

Eben-Emael and the Albert Canal bridges were tackled by the Luftwaffe's airborne troops in spectacular style. The Eben-Emael attack stole the show; it was one of the most daring exploits of the Second World War. The glider-borne soldiers who were dropped right on top of the fort were as heavily laden as any Tommy on the Somme in 1916 – but the deadweight they carried was made up of hollow-charge blocks of TNT. The men used these charges to crack open gun turrets, blind observation slits and domes, and block machine-gun embrasures with rubble. By noon on 11 May the assault pioneers had effectively drawn the teeth of Eben-Emael, whose commandant surrendered. By this time Reichenau's armour was romping across the Albert Canal and the Belgian main line of defence had been torn open. Fighting tenaciously, the Belgian forces fell back to join hands with the dutifully advancing French and British.

By 15 May the Allied line was in position and the first main clashes with Bock's army group had occurred. They amply justified Bock's fears that the right-wing punch through the Low Countries might have been excessively weakened, for Reichenau's attacks on that day were handled very roughly indeed. The French repulsed him at Gembloux and the British

at Louvain, and Reichenau was forced to pull back and start
planning a deliberate, set-piece attack. But this proved unnecessary. North of Namur the Allied line was holding up well – but
to the south the incredible had happened. Kleist's *Panzergruppe*
had debouched from the Ardennes and had smashed through
the 'hinge' of the Allied front, driving across the Meuse around
Sedan.

This famous episode does not need a full description here.
The advance through the Ardennes to Sedan took Guderian
from dawn on 10 May to evening on 12 May, and the Meuse
was crossed on the thirteenth. But even in this short time
differences of opinion had cropped up between Kleist and
Guderian. On the second day of the advance Guderian had had
to argue Kleist out of detaching 10th Panzer Division to
intercept an (apocryphal) advance by French cavalry. And
fresh arguments soon followed once the Meuse was crossed.

Guderian's XIX Corps was not the first to get across. This
honour went to XV Corps under General Hermann Hoth, and
out in the lead was Erwin Rommel's 7th Panzer Division.
Rommel pushed light forces across the Meuse at Houx, north
of Dinant, late on 12 May, and reinforced them the following
day while Guderian's men were crossing at Sedan. A third
crossing – at Monthermé, made by General Georg-Hans
Reinhardt's XLI Corps – ran into stiff resistance and made
slow progress at first, but this mattered little. By 14 May the
Panzer generals – ably assisted by precision work from the
Luftwaffe's Stukas – were on the west bank of the Meuse. The
question now was how to keep the ball rolling.

Guderian's first task was to push south to the high ground
at Stonne and set up a blocking force – a 'hard shoulder' which
would stop any French counter-attacks from carving into the
southern side of the corridor that he now proposed to push deep
into the Allied flank. At the same time he was anxious to
enlarge the bridgehead as much as possible. On 14 May, 1st
and 2nd Panzer Divisions swung to the west while 10th Panzer
headed south. Guderian also knew that he could not proceed
with a full-scale breakout to the west until the infantry took
over, lining the walls of the 'Panzer corridor' and freeing the

armoured units for further advances. At this point Kleist intervened again, calling for a halt. Fast talking by Guderian convinced him that another twenty-four hours of advance were
needed to create enough room for the infantry. And on 16 May
the great dash to the Channel got under way with 1st and 2nd
Panzer arriving at Montcornet, over 20 miles further west,
at the same time as 8th Panzer from Reinhardt's corps. What
wiseacres in the British press began to call 'the Bulge' had
begun its deadly work. The drive to the Channel had begun.

FROM THE MEUSE TO DUNKIRK

Right from the start the sweep of the German 'sickle' was jeopardized by doubts at the top. On 17 May Kleist and Guderian clashed head-on. The *Panzergruppe* commander was furious when he found out how far Guderian had got and he turned down all pleas for an immediate resumption of the advance. Guderian offered his resignation and Kleist accepted it – but on Rundstedt's orders General List of 12th Army intervened and Guderian was authorized to proceed with a 'reconnaissance in force'. As Guderian chose to employ two Panzer divisions for the job, his 'reconnaissance in force' was a resounding success. On 18 May the Oise was crossed and St Quentin taken. On the nineteenth the Somme was crossed near Péronne. On the twentieth Amiens, Albert, and Abbéville fell in rapid succession and the spearhead battalion of 2nd Panzer Division pushed through Noyelles and reached the Channel. Guderian's thrusting tactics had worked wonders. Despite the caution of its commander, the *Panzergruppe* had sliced the Allied front in two.

Kleist's hesitation, however, was nothing to the way in which Hitler's nerve cracked after the reports came in that Guderian was across the Meuse. Even though it was known that the Allies had fallen into the German trap in Belgium, even though the 'impenetrable barrier' of the Ardennes and the Meuse had been proved a myth, Hitler could not believe his own success. On 17 and 18 May he astonished Brauchitsch and Halder by 'raging and screaming' about a non-existent French threat to the southern flank of the 'bulge'. 'He won't have any part in continuing the drive westward,' noted Halder on 18 May. As it turned out, Hitler's panicky attempts to freeze the advance were rendered null and void by the sheer pace of Guderian's divisions, and on 20 May he was only too pleased to change his tune when OKW and OKH finally realized what had been accomplished. 'Führer is beside himself with joy. Talks in words of highest appreciation of the German Army and its leadership,' noted Jodl.

Attention naturally focuses on Guderian when examining these tense days, responsible as he was for the extreme left of the German sweep. But further to the north an equally amazing performance was being put up by Rommel and 7th Panzer Division. Rommel, it will be recalled, crossed the Meuse in the Dinant sector, at Houx, on the thirteenth. Fighting his way out of the bridgehead on the fourteenth and fifteenth, Rommel then proceeded to get away with what was certainly the most daring performance made by any single Panzer division to that date. As night fell on 16 May he was preparing to storm the French fortifications (loosely referred to in German accounts as the 'Maginot Line extension') west of Clairfayts. This was accomplished at lightning speed, with Rommel's Panzers firing salvos to the left and right on the move. Then 7th Panzer Division set off on an epic thirty-mile thrust deep into the French rear, through Avesnes, through Landrecies, across the River Sambre, to Le Cateau. It was an act of sheer military effrontery : a salient thirty miles long and barely two miles wide – but it threw the French troops on the northern side of the German 'bulge' into the wildest confusion. There was hardly time to disarm the hundreds of surrendering French soldiers, let alone round them up ; and Rommel's column ground on its way, with the tank commanders bellowing '*A droit ! A droit !*' to the Frenchmen in a vain attempt to keep the road clear. By the evening of the seventeenth Rommel had secured his position at Le Cateau and by 0500 hours on the twentieth his leading

Panzer regiment had pushed on past Cambrai and was in position south of Arras.

Then, on 21 May, came the counter-blow which had always been likely: an attack by Allied armour against the over-stretched Panzer divisions. It swept south and east from Vimy Ridge, north of Arras, and the whole weight of it fell on Rommel's division. His anti-tank gunners found to their dismay that their standard 37mm guns could not penetrate the massive armour of the lumbering British 'Matildas' and there was considerable panic until Rommel restored the situation by personally seeing to it that every available gun was brought into action against the British tanks. This was the first time that the massive 88mm anti-aircraft gun was used against tanks. Rommel's coolness saved the day for 7th Panzer at Arras, although he was considerably helped by the indecision and piecemeal tactics used by his opponents. But the latter fact does not detract from his achievement in staving off the sudden threat to the 'Panzer corridor'.

With the Channel reached and the northern flank shored up at Arras, Guderian's Panzer divisions swung northwards along the French coast to clear the Channel ports: Boulogne, Calais, and Dunkirk. It soon became clear that the distance covered by the *Panzergruppe* since the crossing of the Meuse had taken little off its cutting edge. Boulogne was invested and attacked by 2nd Panzer on 22 and 23 May, Calais by 10th Panzer. Further inland, Reinhardt's corps pushed a bridgehead across the Aa Canal, barely eighteen miles from Dunkirk. And then came one of the most momentous orders of the war: the notorious 'halt order' from Supreme HQ, which pinned down the Panzer divisions for two vital days and let the British start their embarkation from Dunkirk.

As befits any major controversy, gallons of argumentative ink have been spilt over who was to blame for the 'halt order', and why it was issued at all. The salient facts are as follows. The order went out only three days after the crisis at Arras and it is quite clear that the latter had caused much agitation. It is also easy to forget that every German general knew that the main battle of France had still to be fought, and that excessive tank losses in Flanders could prove disastrous in the long run. What is certain is that Hitler visited Rundstedt at Army Group 'A' headquarters on the morning of 24 May, and that Rundstedt asked for a halt to let the infantry close up on the line pegged out by the Panzers. Hitler agreed. Army Group 'B' would now carry the main weight of the offensive against the Allied troops in the Dunkirk pocket. There was another factor : Göring, who persuaded Hitler that the Luftwaffe could smash the Allies by itself. This was Nazi court politics in action, for Göring was genuinely concerned that the magnificent successes won by the Army would put his Luftwaffe in the shade. So it was that the 'halt order' was allowed to ride, despite the frantic pleas of Brauchitsch and Halder that Bock's forces already had a set-piece battle on their hands and simply did not possess the mobile forces which alone could chew through the Allied perimeter.

The 'halt order' ran for forty-eight hours, during which time the British and French had enough time to strengthen the inner defences around Dunkirk itself, and round up the 'little ships' for the improvized embarkation which was now clearly essential. The magnificent defence of Lille by the French 1st Army was, however, a factor of equal importance. But on 27 May, the day after the 'halt order' was lifted, the Belgian Army capitulated, allowing Army Group 'B' to drive straight for Dunkirk and cut off the French in Lille. By the twenty-ninth the German ring was clamped tightly round Dunkirk, but could not reach the beaches. Nor could the Luftwaffe stop the embarkations. By 4 June, when Dunkirk finally fell, 338,226 Allied troops had been withdrawn from the port and the beaches – all of whom would be able to fight again, and whose escape robbed the *Sichelschnitt* plan of its most potent motive : annihilation.

A resounding victory it remained, however, in that France had been robbed of all Allied troops and must now face the Wehmacht alone, trying to hold an improvized front with sadly weakened forces. For a week, German divisions had been pulled out of Flanders and regrouped along the Somme for the new offensive which would bring France to her knees for ever.

THE BATTLE OF FRANCE

The way in which the OKW set about the final phase of the campaign in the West was a competent use of initiative, experience, and flexibility. It had taken the Wehrmacht ten days to rip open the Allied front and plunge through to the Channel ; and this final series of operations took little longer. This time all three German army groups were used, being brought into play successively. Army Group 'B' would strike first, on the lower Somme ; then Army Group 'A', across the Aisne ; and finally Army Group 'C', emerging from the Siegfried Line to tackle the Maginot Line defences and help bottle up the surviving French forces in the eastern sector.

Big changes were made in the development of the armour. Three *Panzergruppen* now replaced the original grouping which had plunged through the Ardennes and across the Meuse. Hoth commanded the first, on the lower Somme ; he was given 5th and 7th Panzer Divisions. In the centre, facing the Péronne-Amiens sector, was Kleist, with 9th, 10th, 3rd, and 4th Panzer Divisions ; and facing the Aisne was Guderian with 1st, 2nd, 6th, and 8th Panzer Divisions. The French had not only frittered away their last chances of concentrating a mobile armoured reserve (latterly in fruitless attacks against the German bridgeheads across the Somme) ; they were now outnumbered overall. The new French C-in-C, Weygand, could only field 71 divisions against the Germans' 143. All he could do was to issue a back-to-the-wall order of the day and hope to stave off a decisive German breakthrough for as long as possible. The French troops fought magnificently and they gave Bock and Kleist plenty of trouble in the opening days of the offensive – but the issue was never in doubt.

Bock and Army Group 'B' opened the play on 5 June, striking across the lower Somme. Here the French held stubbornly for forty-eight hours before Rommel and 7th Panzer made another of their superb breakthroughs and set off for the lower Seine at full throttle. It was a very different story with Kleist's *Panzergruppe*, trying to break out of the bridgeheads at Amiens and Péronne. Kleist's forces hammered away at the French for four days but had got nowhere by the time that Army Group 'A' launched its attack on 9 June. Here, attacking on both sides of Rethel, Guderian was held up for twenty-four hours before breaking out south of the Aïsne and heading for the Marne. OKH and OKW made the intelligent decision to regard Guderian's success as a 'tin-opener' for Kleist's *Panzergruppe*, which was promptly transferred to Guderian's sector. Here Kleist's group scored rapid successes and it soon became clear that this would be the decisive front : eight Panzer divisions were boring forwards on both sides of Rheims.

The two stars of the Battle of France were Rommel and Guderian – Rommel for the record-breaking distances covered by his division, Guderian (again) for his astuteness in overriding the vagueness of the orders from the High Commands which only caught up with him long after the most recent advances had made them obsolete. Mention should also be made of General Rudolf Kirchner, commander of 1st Panzer Division, which spearheaded Guderian's drive across the Marne and the Saône to the Swiss border at Ponterlier.

Rommel clinched the campaign in the West with two remarkable successes against key Channel ports. By 9 June he had reached the Seine at Elbeuf, covering forty-five miles in his last day's advance, only to find that the Seine bridges had all been blown. He then made a right-angled turn to the north-west and immediately roared off towards Fécamp and St. Valéry. On the tenth he covered over sixty miles and reached the coast. On the eleventh he moved against St. Valéry and on the twelfth he took the port, where for the first time in the history of armoured warfare tanks and anti-aircraft guns traded fire with warships. Rommel's men rounded up the shattered remains of the French IX Corps and the British 51st Highland Division, together with its commander General Fortune, in whose company Rommel proudly posed for a victory photograph. After a five-day respite 7th Panzer was switched back to the lower Seine once more. Covering an incredible 150 miles in a single day, his forces ringed Cherbourg on 18 June and the garrison surrendered the following day. Since 10 May 7th Panzer had taken nearly 100,000 prisoners, over 300 guns, 450 armoured fighting vehicles, and transport numbering 700. Its own losses were as low as 42 knocked-out tanks and total manpower losses (killed, wounded, and missing) under 3,000.

Similar pace was maintained at the other end of the front by Guderian. On 12 June his *Panzergruppe* took Chalons-sur-Marne ; on the thirteenth Vitry-le-François ; on the fourteenth Chaumont ; on the fifteenth Langres, Gray-sur-Saône and Bar-le-Duc. On the sixteeth it broke out across the Saône and took Besançon ; and on 17 June it reached Pontarlier on the Swiss frontier. Guderian proudly radioed OKW when Pontarlier fell and was delighted to receive the incredulous signal : 'Your signal based on an error. Assume you mean Pontailler-sur-Saône.' 'No error,' ran Guderian's reply. 'Am myself in Pontarlier on Swiss border.' This, Guderian later recalled with a touch of thoroughly justifiable complacency in his memoirs, 'finally satisfied the distrustful OKW.'

Like Rommel on the lower Seine, Guderian now ordered a right-angled turn which sent his *Panzergruppe* striking north-eastward into the Vosges and Alsace, operating in close touch with the attacks being made by Leeb's Army Group 'C' against the Maginot Line. Kirchner's 1st Panzer Division joined hands with General Friedrich Dollmann's 7th Army on 19 June, trapping 400,000 French troops in the Vosges. Meanwhile Kleist's forces were swarming southward towards Lyons, which was occupied on 20 June.

Weygand's front along the Somme and the Aisne had never been anything more than a crash barrier. There was nothing behind it. The French Government was forced to agree to the abandonment of Paris, which the Germans occupied on the fourteenth. Reynaud fell and the defeatist (or, as he always put it, realist) Marshal Pétain took over with one intention and one alone : to stop the agony and arrange an armistice. This was signed at Compiègne on 22 June and the shooting finally stopped on 25 June.

The Wehrmacht had destroyed the challenge of France and all her Continental Allies and had sent the British Army packing with the loss of all the heavy equipment which it had taken to France. The terms which France was forced to swallow in return for peace were intended to keep her prostrate for ever. As Hitler's generals enjoyed their new decorations and promotions and luxuriated in Paris during the magnificent summer of 1940 it really seemed for a while that every one of their fears had been laid. Poland had been destroyed and so had the Western Allies who had gone to war to save her. The German Army had won a series of victories without parallel in its history. Now, surely, there was nothing left to fight about, and nothing to do but bask in the glory.

But it soon became apparent that there had been disastrous deficiencies in the planning of the war, which not only continued but branched out into the nightmare of war on two fronts, which in June 1940 had seemed so totally impossible.

THE BEST ANTI-TANK DITCH IN THE WORLD

Not until France fell did the OKW and OKH planners realize what an empty victory had been won. The whole idea of the campaign in the West had originally been to end the war. This could only be done by defeating France *and* Britain. But the campaign ended up as a one-sided vendetta against France, symbolized by the humiliating stage-management which made the French delegates sign the surrender of their country in the railway carriage where Marshal Foch had accepted Germany's ·surrender in 1918. With absurd complacency, Hitler and his military experts sat back and waited for the British to call it a day. When the British declined to do so, then – and only then – did planning begin for the conquest of Britain, amid much pious lamenting from Hitler over what a tragedy the whole thing was.

The unpleasant truth was that because of this head-in-the-sand attitude about how the British would react, all the brain-work that had gone into *Sichelschnitt* had only produced a house without a roof. The Meuse, the Oise, the Aa Canal, the Somme, the Aisne, the Seine – these had been easy obstacles. But by the time of the French armistice no more planning had been put into how to cross the English Channel than into how to cross the Volga – or, for that matter, the Nile or the Ganges. What was amazing was the speed with which *Seelöwe* – 'Sea

Lion', the plan to invade Britain – was subsequently rushed into existence as a serious military proposition.

Hitler was, of course, the chief culprit for the delays caused by this defective reasoning – but he was not the only culprit. Not one of his professional advisers – Army, Navy, or Luftwaffe – had pressed the point of what must be done in the event of continued British resistance. Instead they started and finished with the obvious difficulties and did nothing whatever to tackle them until far too late in the day. If Eisenhower and his team had gone about planning the invasion of Europe the way the German High Command behaved over *Seelöwe*, the D-Day landings would probably not have been made before 1950 – if then.

The first vague moves towards formulating the *Seelöwe* plan were made on 2 July, when an OKW directive ordered preparations to be made for a possible invasion of Britain – if and when. On 11 July Hitler talked with Raeder about an invasion, and the Grand-Admiral issued an instant *nolle prosequi*. The German Navy had taken a severe mauling during the Norwegian campaign and simply did not have anything like the number of escorts which would be needed. Paradoxically – one might almost say pathetically – Raeder went on to affirm that an invasion of Britain was unnecessary. Naval and air blockade would suffice to strangle Britain – a thesis which bears an uncomfortable resemblance to Göring's boast that the Luftwaffe could wipe out the Dunkirk pocket on its own. With Brauchitsch and Halder two days later Hitler took a more evasive line, giving Halder the comfortable impression that the Führer did not really want to tackle Britain head-on. 'With German blood we would achieve something from which only Japan, America, and others would benefit.'

On 16 July Hitler moved a little closer by issuing his *Directive No. 16*, ordering preparations for an invasion of Britain – again with the proviso 'if necessary' – to be completed by mid-August under the code-name *Seelöwe*. And on the nineteenth he rose in the Reichstag to make his celebrated 'peace offer' speech with the punch-line: 'I can see no reason why this war must go on.'

For Hitler's generals, however, 19 July 1940 was especially memorable as prize-giving day. Twelve top generals were presented with their field-marshals' batons – a large-scale largesse without precedent in German history. (Even the legendary Ludendorff had never been promoted Field-marshal). Keitel and Brauchitsch headed the list for the German Army. Next came the three army group commanders, Bock, Rundstedt, and Leeb, and four army commanders : Kluge, List, Reichenau, and Witzleben. The Luftwaffe too was honoured. Kesselring and Sperrle got their batons and so did Erhard Milch, former Secretary of State for Air under Göring and chief of aircraft supply and production. Göring himself kept his position as the top-ranking officer of the Reich : Hitler named him 'Reich Marshal'. (William Shirer, who witnessed the whole scene, noted sardonically : 'Hitler turned around and handed him a box with whatever insignia a *Reichsmarschall* wears. Göring took the box, and his boyish pride and satisfaction were almost touching, old murderer that he is. He could not deny himself a sneaking glance under the cover of the lid.')

These promotions are of special interest as they reveal the mixture of carrot and stick with which Hitler treated his generals. Keitel's promotion was the rewarding of a good dog ; Brauchitsch's promotion unavoidable because of his position of C-in-C, Army. The leaders of Göring's pet, the Luftwaffe, were also understandable. But Halder was pointedly omitted. Also conspicuous by their absence were the *Panzergruppe* commanders. The German Army was still at the stage when the Panzer force was regarded as a service department for the individual field armies. And the choice of army commanders was interesting: two from Army Group 'A' (Kluge and List), one from Army Group 'B' (Reichenau), and one from Army Group 'C' (Witzleben).

The British rejection of the 'peace offer' of 19 July, however, came virtually within the hour. Now the new field-marshals and the generals were faced with the reality of what Britain's obduracy must mean. *Seelöwe* must be worked out in detail after all.

In fact, OKH had completed its provisional plan two days

before, within twenty-four hours of Hitler's *Directive No. 16* being issued. It was a lavish plan, apparently well thought-out, but it was also thoroughly hypocritical because neither Brauchitsch nor Halder believed that there was the faintest chance of its ever being ordered into operation.

Rundstedt's Army Group 'A' was to spearhead the invasion. He would be given two armies : General Ernst Busch's 16th Army and General Adolf Strauss's 9th Army. The assault wave on the first day would be made up of ten divisions. Busch, with six divisions, would land between Ramsgate and Bexhill ; Strauss, with four divisions, would land between Brighton and the Isle of Wight. Further to the west, Reichenau's 6th Army would go in at Lyme Bay with three divisions to over-stretch the British still further. Six Panzer divisions and three motor-ized divisions would go in with the second wave, once the beach-heads had been won. Brauchitsch envisaged a final build-up to a strength of thirty-nine divisions plus two airborne divisions and told Raeder that the whole operation would be over in a month. But Raeder, faced with landing forces along a 200-mile front, had other ideas.

He spoke out at the conference with Hitler on 21 July but Hitler backed the Army's broad-front plan. Raeder pointed out that he could only lay on enough shipping to cover a landing on a much narrower front, from Dover to Eastbourne. He used every argument he could, even claiming that he would have to commandeer every barge and transport plying on Germany's inland waterways – an act which would ruin the internal trans-port system of the Reich. He repeated all this at another conference on 31 July, but in the directives of the following day the broad-front attack survived. However, the 1 August directives covered one point on which both Army and Navy were agreed. The Royal Air Force must be destroyed as a fight-ing force and the Luftwaffe assured of total control over the Narrow Seas. And a date was set by which all must be ready : 15 September.

Now there occurred a series of collisions between Army and Navy over the basic dilemma of the Wehrmacht as its leaders buckled down to the details of landing in southern England.

The Navy rejected the wide-front plan because of the danger to the invasion fleet ; the Army rejected the narrow-front plan because, as Halder acidly pointed out on 7 August, 'I might just as well put the troops that have landed straight through a mincing machine.' On 10 August Brauchitsch tried a compromise, still rejecting the narrow-front plan but offering to drop the Lyme Bay attack in order to shorten the front. Still Raeder held out : even this new front would be too much for the Navy's resources.

On 13 August Phase 1 of *Seelöwe* was implemented with the beginning of the first mass Luftwaffe forays across the Channel. To the rising tempo of the air battle which reached crescendo a month later, the wrangling and arguing went on as the days slipped by. 16 August: the Lyme Bay landing is definitely dropped. 27 August: *Seelöwe* assault modified to four main areas along the coastline Selsey Bill – Folkestone. 30 August: OKH issues instructions for the landings to the commanding generals. 1 September : all shipping earmarked for the crossing is set in motion towards its embarkation-points. And then, on 3 September, came yet another OKW directive setting D-Day at 21 September and the date for the executive order as 11 September.

Like *Fall Gelb*, however, *Seelöwe* was repeatedly postponed and the reasons are interesting. Göring's assumption of 'personal command' prevented OKW from getting an accurate assessment of the exact state of the air battle over Britain. There was gross over-confidence in the disruption of civilian morale in London. The superb summer of 1940 was breaking up and the Navy was having trouble in massing the invasion fleet. Hitler postponed the invasion on the tenth and again on the fourteenth. The onus was passed back, once again, to the Luftwaffe, which was given three more days – until the seventeenth – in which to finish off the RAF once and for all and stampede London into a panic-stricken exodus from the bombing. The intense air fighting on 15 September, in which not a single bomber formation got through to London unmolested, proved that the RAF was still in the ring and, according to most reports, as strong as ever. But this was not all. RAF

Bomber Command, smashing away at the clustering barges in the invasion ports, was drawing blood at an alarming rate. It was enough.

German Naval War Diary, 17 September 1940 : 'The Führer decides to postpone *Seelöwe* indefinitely.'

Two days later Hitler gave another order : to stop the build-up of the invasion fleet and disperse the existing flotillas to save further losses. The troops, however, stayed in position for another month until, on 12 October, a Führer Directive formally stood them down and ordered their dispersal. 'Should the invasion be reconsidered in the spring or early summer of 1941, orders for a renewal of operational readiness will be issued later.'

The Wehrmacht had met its match – but not because of the fighting qualities of the Luftwaffe in the Battle of Britain. That battle could have been won. *Seelöwe* stood revealed as a paper tiger because of the half-baked objectives with which Hitler had gone to war with the Western Allies. That was the strategic reality. But Hitler could also have claimed that his military chiefs had let him down badly by not working out solutions to the long-term problems created by their short-term victories.

Only one thing can be said in favour of the generals and admirals who argued *Seelöwe* back into the files at OKW. They are certainly to blame for not having commenced planning early enough, but they recognized the impossible when they saw it, and so, for once, did Hitler.

Not that this prevented him from almost immediately laying his plans for the biggest gamble of all : the attack on Soviet Russia.

THE BIRTH OF BARBAROSSA

One can search all the archives and every deposition made by Hitler's generals after the collapse of their country in 1945, and be overwhelmed with professions of horror which Hitler's determination to attack Russia aroused in the leaders of the German Army. The fact remains that it was no more of a surprise than his expansionist policy between 1934 and 1939. That had been clearly set out in *Mein Kampf*: which had been one of Europe's best-sellers for years. So it was with 'Barbarossa', the definitive code-name given to the attempt to break Soviet Russia as Poland, Norway, Denmark, Holland, Belgium and France had been broken. The generals in the know had been told where they would be going even before the Polish campaign began.

On 22 August 1939 Hitler had held a conference at the Berghof. It was a pep-talk for the Wehrmacht commanders and their staffs, neatly timed to cash in on the feelings of relief inspired by the news that Ribbentrop had gone to Moscow to sign a pact with Russia, and in which Hitler strove to inspire his generals with his own 'savage resolution'. And he summed up his harangue with the words: 'War must come in my life-time. My pact was only meant to stall for time and, gentlemen, to Russia will happen just what I have practised with Poland – we will crush the Soviet Union.'

In August 1939 this was not only bombast but frightening bombast, for it meant one thing and one thing alone : war on two fronts. Thirteen months later, however, despite the calling-off of *Seelöwe*, not even the most pessimistic general could deny that Germany's position was radically different. And in fact – unlike *Seelöwe* – preliminary planning for the Russian gamble had been afoot for weeks.

As far as OKW was concerned, the first crucial date was 29 July 1940, when Jodl briefed a hand-picked nucleus team of planners under terms of the strictest secrecy. Hitler had already made enquiries as to whether or not the attack would be possible in the autumn of 1940 and he was prepared to accept the firm 'no' he was given. Raeder and Göring, let into the secret on 31 July, were told that he was planning to go ahead in May 1941. Detailed planning was to commence under General Marcks. Immediate technical problems raised their heads. In the euphoria of the victory in France, OKW had set in motion preliminary demobilization. Now, however, the Army must be raised to over 180 divisions ; the number of Panzer divisions must be doubled and the motorized units increased – in all, the creation of some forty brand-new divisions. In September and October Bock, Kluge and List were transferred to eastern Germany, followed in short order by Brauchitsch and the OKH, which returned from Fontainebleau to the main OKH base at Zossen, south of Berlin. Leeb and his staff were also recalled to Germany in this period. Operation *Aufbau Ost*, the eastern build-up, had begun.

The most striking aspect of the planning of the Russian campaign is the attitude of Brauchitsch and Halder. Hitler made it clear that he regarded this campaign as the decisive stroke of the war, not to be set off at half-cock. The OKH clearly respected this and gave of their best during the long months of planning. Their bedrock professionalism was deeply involved, for this campaign could only be won by the Army. They reckoned the job could be done in five months, as Hitler demanded. And they were ready to swallow Hitler's argument that the menacing attitude of Russia since the spring of 1940 – the Baltic states gobbled up, Rumania forced to give up

Bessarabia, and all manner of vague diplomatic accusations and threats besides – left the Reich with little choice.

So it was that on 18 December 1940 Hitler signed *Führer Directive No. 21* – 'Barbarossa'. Three Army Groups – North, Centre, and South – would attack on a huge front between the Baltic and Black Seas. The objective was the annihilation of the Red Army in Panzer battles which must be brought on as far west as possible. Two snags were certainly left unresolved. The first was the brief of destroying the country's will to resist. In previous campaigns this had been achieved, but Britain had proved the exception to the rule. What would happen if, despite all victories in the field, Russia managed to survive a five-months' battering ? The second worry was strategic. Where would the Wehrmacht stop ? The only objective mentioned in the 'Barbarossa' Directive was no answer : the 'A-A' line (an arbitrary line between Archangel on the White Sea and Astrakhan on the Caspian) offered no natural defensible front. Both these questions were left in the air.

Far more serious, however, were the events of September 1940 to May 1941, which created an entirely new German theatre in the Mediterranean and drained off energy, man-power, and weapons from the decisive struggle in Russia. In addition, this new distraction served to delay the invasion of Russia by a month. This would push Hitler's five-month dead-line into late autumn – and Hitler had already refused to sanction the mass preparation of winter equipment on the grounds that it would disrupt the German war economy.

And it all came about because of the hopeless inadequacies of Mussolini's armed forces, which in the space of three months had managed to get themselves disastrously beaten wherever they fought. True to his pledge to come to Mussolinin's aid 'even if the whole world were against him', Hitler watered down the Wehrmacht on the eve of its greatest trial.

The Norwegian campaign had forced him to keep German forces stationed at the North Cape. These new Mediterranean entanglements meant that the Wehrmacht was now stretched from the North Cape to the Sahara Desert, and from the Atlantic to the plains of Russia.

HELP FOR THE DUCE

Mussolini had gone to war on 10 June 1940 and had wasted no time in sending two armies across the Alps to tackle southern France. The lamentable performance put up by his forces earned him the derision of the world – not for the first time. And it caused the gravest concern to Hitler and OKW.

For years Mussolini had been boasting of the new frontiers which his 'second Roman Empire' intended to get – by force if necessary. They boiled down to a replacement of British preponderance by Italian in the entire Mediterranean. And they were a profound embarrassment to Hitler because he wanted to let sleeping dogs lie in the Balkans and the Mediterranean. Raeder thought differently: he saw the Mediterranean as the one theatre where the British could be given a decisive beating. OKW had laid plans for one very important prize: Gibraltar. This was to be accomplished by Operation *Felix,* for which General Franco's kind cooperation was assiduously sought during the autumn of 1940. Hitler wanted Franco to allow free passage for a German armoured corps to assault Gibraltar from the landward. Franco, however, was not to be pressured into jumping on the Axis bandwagon and Operation *Felix* remained in cold storage.

When it seemed that the German airborne assault on Britain could end in no other way but the invasion and conquest of the island, Mussolini ordered an invasion of his own out of sheer pique. This was Graziani's invasion of Egypt, scheduled to cross the frontier on the day promised for the German landings in southern England. Graziani's forces lumbered into Egypt on 13 September, advanced sixty cautious miles to Sidi Barrani, sat down, and hastily dug themselves in. And there they stayed, for all Mussolini's impatient urgings from Rome. It was not an auspicious beginning.

The Duce hoped for better luck against Greece, which he proposed to attack from Italy's new trans-Adriatic province of Albania. Personal rivalry impelled him here, for he was furious that the Germans had sent a large military mission to Rumania. 'Hitler always faces me with a *fait accompli*,' he sulked. 'This time I am going to pay him back in his own coin. He will find out from the papers that I have occupied Greece.' To his son-in-law Count Ciano, Italian Foreign Minister, the Duce subsequently commented 'I shall send in my resignation as an Italian if anyone objects to our fighting the Greeks.' He did have the fleeting pleasure of telling Hitler 'Führer, we are on the march !' at Florence station on 28 October ; but, beginning on 3 November, spirited Greek counter-attacks drove the Italian forces helter-skelter back across the frontier and kept up the pressure on Albanian soil. On 11 November exultant students in occupied Paris paraded in celebration of the Greek victories ; and placards were put up on the Italo-French frontier which read : 'French territory – Greeks, do not pursue Italians past this point.' On the same day as the parade in Paris, 11 November, the British Fleet Air Arm sank three Italian battleships in Taranto harbour.

Worse was to come. On 8 December General Wavell, the British commander in Egypt, launched what he cautiously described to pressmen as a 'heavy raid' against the Italian army at Sidi Barrani. On 14 December the tiny British and Empire forces swept the defeated Italians back into Libya and promptly laid siege to the fortress of Bardia. By 21 January 1941 they had pressed on to the west and taken Tobruk. The Duce's armies had reached the rock-bottom of military insolvency in five disastrous months.

Time, in fact, for the Wehrmacht to move in and pick up the pieces before the initiative in the Mediterranean passed irretrievably to the British. By the end of December 1940 General Geissler's X *Fliegerkorps* had arrived in Sicily, its mission being to command the sea lanes in the central Mediterranean and begin a serious bombardment of Malta. Geissler's bomber crews made their début on 10 January 1940, badly damaging the British aircraft-carrier *Illustrious* and forcing her to quit the Mediterranean for extensive repairs. From then on until March Malta was kept under constant German air bombardment and the diminutive fighter establishment on the island was steadily whittled away.

During this period far more Axis supplies were landed at Tripoli – and a legend was born. Hitler had decided that he must send a German force to North Africa to keep the British out of Tripoli. Such were the origins of the Afrika Korps, of which Erwin Rommel was appointed commander on 6 February. After stopping off at Catania, Sicily, to confer with Geissler, Rommel landed at Tripoli on 12 February. He had an awkward brief, to put it mildly. He was to remain subordinate to the Italian commander, General Gariboldi, but was strictly enjoined by OKH not to let his force be parcelled out with other Italian units. A German group it was and a German group it was to remain : 5th Light Division to start with, soon to be joined by 15th Panzer. Within hours of first landing on African soil, Rommel was flying to the front to familiarize himself with the terrain. His first troops landed at Tripoli on 14 February and within twenty-six hours Rommel had them in the front line he intended to form at Sirte.

Ironically, the threat to Tripoli had evaporated. General O'Connor, the brains behind the British conquest of Libya, had certainly wished to push on to Tripoli. But the obsession with pulling desert-wise troops out of the line and packing them off to help the Greeks against the Italians was the dominant factor now. The replacements sent up to hold the British front line were of greatly inferior quality, in both combat experience and equipment. It was unfortunate for them that facing them was

one of the most resourceful, unorthodox and daring commanders of mobile forces the war had produced to date.

After satisfying himself that there was no immediate threat
to Tripoli, Rommel began a series of cautious, shadow-boxing
advances further and further east along the coast road. Every
contact with the British, however slight, provoked a withdrawal on their part and on 19 March Rommel flew to OKW
to report. He was told bluntly that there was no question of any
rapid counter-moves being made in the near future. Nor would
he be getting any more troops for some time. After 15th Panzer
joined his command at the end of May it would be appropriate
to start considering the recapture of Benghazi. Thoroughly
disgruntled at the total lack of interest shown by Brauchitsch
and Halder, Rommel returned to North Africa with his mind
made up. He would proceed as he and Guderian had done
after crossing the Meuse.

Before his flight to Germany he had arranged for an attack
on the British position at El Agheila. This went in at dawn on
24 March and it was a complete success. Following up hard
and fast, Rommel bounced the British out of their strong
position at Mersa el Brega on 31 March and kept going, driving
on to take Agedabia on 2 April. By 3 April, reports from
reconnaissance aircraft had told him what he had already
sensed – the British were streaming eastward as fast as they
could. Rommel had correctly decided that Cyrenaica could not
be held by anyone if an enemy pulled off a decisive stroke in
the open desert inland. He therefore made the daring decision
to expand his initial successes into a runaway conquest, the way
O'Connor had done in December 1940-January 1941. He split
his tiny forces into three prongs : one stabbing along the coast
road to Benghazi, one directly across the desert through Msus,
and the third swinging deep inland. Benghazi, which Rommel
was scheduled to think about attacking after the end of May
according to OKW, fell on 4 April. On 7 April Rommel's three
prongs closed together at Mechili. Derna fell on the eighth
Equally hasty but ill-advised attacks were repulsed by the
defenders of Tobruk on the tenth, and the siege of the place

began. By the end of the month his forward reconnaissance forces had taken Sollum, Halfaya, and Capuzzo and Axis troops once more stood on the Egyptian border. Apart from Tobruk, Rommel had got the whole of Cyrenaica back for Mussolini.

By the time that the spearheads of the Afrika Korps reached the Egyptian frontier, however, another Wehrmacht offensive had been launched to solve the situation in the Balkans once and for all. Operation 'Marita' was the code-name for a German invasion of Greece. This was a forestalling move, provoked by the original Italian invasion which had made it inevitable that sooner or later the British would come to the aid of the Greeks and be provided with bases from which bombing raids could be made against Germany's vital sources of oil at Ploesti in Rumania. But the situation was made more complex by a classic Hitlerian brainstorm. To block possible Soviet ambitions in the Balkans, Bulgaria, Rumania and Yugoslavia had been pressured into signing the 'Tripartite Pact' between Germany, Italy and Japan. But on 27 March Yugoslavia broke loose. A *coup d'état* in Belgrade repudiated the supine activities of Prince Paul's government – and Hitler erupted with an outpouring of vicious spite such as had not been heard since his rantings against the 'pygmy race' of the Czechs in 1938. He immediately ordered the destruction of Yugoslavia under the utterly descriptive code-name 'Punishment'. It was to proceed simultaneously with 'Marita' ; and 'Barbarossa' was to be postponed four weeks in consequence.

'Punishment' would begin for the Yugoslavs with a mass bombing raid on Belgrade on 6 April – Palm Sunday. The ground offensive was entrusted to General von Weichs and 2nd Army, striking from Austria and Hungary ; *Panzergruppe* Kleist, striking from Rumania and Bulgaria ; and Field-Marshal List with 12th Army, also striking from Bulgaria. This was a monstrous force to throw against the down-at-heel, if resolute, Yugoslav armies. As usual, German air supremacy was assured, this time by General Löhr's *Luftflotte* IV. The destruction of the Yugoslav Army took just ten days, with the country's surrender being signed in Belgrade on 17 April.

The assault on Yugoslavia made the Allied defence of Greece hopeless, for it was part of the brief of both Kleist and List that they see to it that all communication between Greece and Yugoslavia was severed in the first days. Wheeling south over the mountains along the Yugoslav-Greek border, the German forces thus detached from the campaign in Yugoslavia turned the Allied positions along the Aliakmon river and the 'Metaxas Line' facing the Bulgarian border.

The two highlights of the campaign really occurred during the retreat to the south, which the German turning movement from Yugoslavia made essential within forty-eight hours. The first was the battle for Mount Olympus, which was won against all adversity by 2nd Panzer Division, advancing on both sides of the mountain, and by 6th Mountain Division, tackling the heights. The second was the rearguard action at Thermopylae in which the Australian and New Zealand troops won sufficient time for the withdrawal to the Peloponnese to be continued. The Greek divisions holding the Albanian front held out to the end ; but by mutual agreement the Greeks surrendered at Salonika on 24 April while the British executed a second Dunkirk from the Peloponnese. By the end of April the last British and Empire troops had left and German mastery of the Balkans was complete.

Hitler was not satisfied, however. He ordered the Luftwaffe to go ahead with Operation 'Mercury' : the conquest of Crete, which would deny the British still more airfields in the central Mediterranean while adding new ones to extend the range of the Luftwaffe. Like the invasion of Norway, 'Mercury' was a unique operation. It was left solely to the German airborne arm, which conquered the island between 20 May and 1 June, but which suffered such heavy losses that it was never able to launch a similar operation again. General Kurt Student's airborne troops suffered 3,714 killed and missing and 2,494 wounded – more casualties than the Wehrmacht had suffered during the entire three weeks' campaign in Yugoslavia and Greece.

So it was that by the first week in June 1941 the heavy forces 'lent' for the purpose of clearing out the Balkans were moving north to resume their places along what would shortly become the Eastern Front. At dawn on 22 June Hitler's boast – 'When Barbarossa begins, the world will hold its breath and make no comment' – would be put to the test.

TO THE GATES OF MOSCOW

The mobile phase of 'Barbarossa' – from 22 June 1941 until 5 December, when the Red Army's counterattack began 'before Moscow – was the last time that the veteran generals worked together in anything like the same combination in which they had begun the war. Although distorted by the vast scale of the Eastern Front, by the way in which much larger forces than had ever been committed were dwarfed by the distances covered, the basic German deployment was very much the same mixture as before.

The main line-up consisted of Army Groups 'North', 'Centre', and 'South', under Leeb, Bock, and Rundstedt respectively. This time, however, each army group had at least one *Panzergruppe* of its own. For Leeb there was *Panzergruppe* IV, commanded by General Erich Höppner, who had commanded a Panzer corps in the West, first under Reichenau during the drive into Belgium, later under Kleist in the Battle of France. The other *Panzergruppe* commanders were all familiar names. Army Group Centre had the biggest concentration of armour, with *Panzergruppe* II (Guderian) and *Panzergruppe* III (Hoth). Army Group South had Kleist's *Panzergruppe* I. An interesting point was the reappearance of Manstein, back in harness and commanding LVI Corps under Höppner.

Far to the north were Dietl's Narvik veterans, reinforced to corps strength now and charged with the capture of Murmansk, the only Russian northern port free of ice all the year round. Bridging the gap between Dietl and Army Group North was Marshal Mannerheim and the Finnish Army, eager to recover the losses of the Winter War. The Wehrmacht had other allies too : there were two Rumanian armies, a Hungarian corps, and a Slovakian corps, all under Rundstedt's overall command. Other foreign contingents which arrived in Russia after the campaign began were three Italian divisions, plus the volunteer Spanish 'Blue Division', courtesy of General Franco.

The original objectives for the three army groups as laid down in the 'Barbarossa' directive were as follows. Leeb : Baltic states/Leningrad; Bock: Smolensk/Leningrad; Rundstedt: Ukraine/Kiev/Crimea. The attainment of these objectives would follow on from the massive battles of annihilation which would destroy the Red Army as a fighting force. But the way in which operations developed caused several crucial changes of plan which radically changed the appearance of 'Barbarossa' – and ruined the chances of decisive victory in 1941.

What happened is simple enough in the telling. The concentrated thrust on Leningrad never came off, although Army Group North did wonders in driving to the outskirts of the city virtually single-handed (it had, moreover, the weakest of the four *Panzergruppen*). In the centre Bock's armour bit off two huge pockets of surrounded Soviet forces, at Bialystok/Minsk and at Smolensk, and arrived at Yelnya on the Desna river, not 200 miles from Moscow. Rundstedt's Army Group South had the hardest initial fighting to do, but it finally succeeded in breaking through the 'Stalin Line' fixed defences and overran the Ukraine south of the Dniepr. At this point Hitler intervened, scrapped the original idea to concentrate on Leningrad, ignored all arguments for a pounce towards Moscow, and ordered the *Panzergruppen* of Army Groups Centre and South to cooperate in the conquest of the Ukraine. Guderian and Kleist wheeled inwards towards each other and finally joined hands east of Kiev, closing the ring behind the massive concentration of Russian forces trying to defend Kiev. Then – and

only then – did Hitler grant permission for the drive on
Moscow. By the time the *Panzergruppen* were back in position
and ready to jump off it was the first week of October.
'Typhoon' was the code-name given to this second phase of
'Barbarossa', and it started well with another gigantic encirclement battle at Vyazma/Bryansk; but when the heavy rains
came the country dissolved in mud and the advance floundered
to a halt. Although the foremost troops, enduring the first
terrible winter frosts in their summer gear, got to within twenty
miles of the Kremlin, they could do no more. And on 5
December Army Group Centre was forced to fight for its life
as the Russian winter counter-offensive began.

Against this overall background the individual performances
of the generals varied considerably and this was not altogether
their fault. As far as close overall control and guidance from
above was concerned, 'Barbarossa' was one of the most dis-
jointed campaigns the Wehrmacht ever fought. To start with,
OKH remained a zero factor throughout. Halder – inveterate
scribbler that he was – admitted this depressing fact in writing.
On 29 June, with the campaign just one week old, he wrote:
'Let us hope that the Commanding Generals of Corps and
Armies will do the right thing without express orders which we
are not allowed to issue because of the Führer's instructions to
[Brauchitsch].' Here was a pretty humiliating admission for
an army chief-of-staff to have to make, even to himself. Such
was the state of abjectness to which Hitler had reduced his own
Army High Command. And the generals did not always do the
right thing. A case in point was Leeb's Army Group North,
which had set a cracking pace in the first week, getting half-way
to Leningrad in the first five days. But then Hoeppner badly
weakened his Panzergruppe by sending his corps commanders,
Manstein and Reinhardt, off in different directions. Concentrated they had worked wonders; separated they bogged down,
giving the Russians time to vamp up a defence for Leningrad
that was just strong enough. Leeb did not intervene to put
things right. Nor did the High Command.

Another example of this inherent weakness in the
Wehrmacht during the 'glory days' of 'Barbarossa' was thrown

up by Army Group Centre. The two Panzer virtuosos, Hoth and Guderian, worked brilliantly together in the battles of encirclement. But Kluge of 4th Army made unceasing attempts to keep Guderian to heel and slow his armour down, and the result was constant friction. As with Leeb, so with Bock. It was the Army Group commander's job to sort out misapprehensions such as this; but Bock did nothing. Brauchitsch and Halder, deprived of the effective control of the armies thanks to Hitler, should have resigned. Instead they chose to stay on and took refuge in bombarding the front-line commanders with nagging points of infuriating detail, instead of shielding the front-line commanders from the importunities of OKW. Yet one thing is to their credit: their attitude to the notorious decrees passed to the Army by OKW. These decrees stated that German soldiers would be absolved from automatic court-martial in the event of 'excesses' committed against Russian prisoners and civilians; and that all Party commissars captured in the field were to be shot out of hand. Brauchitsch could not quash the issuing of these decrees (which helped bring Keitel and Jodl to the gallows after the war); but he did pass on the civilian-prisoner decree with a postscript that it was only to be carried out if there were no danger of discipline suffering. For generals like Guderian such a hint was enough and the order was not passed down the line to the divisions.

For all these weaknesses, however, 'Barbarossa' was carried to within an ace of success by the German troops and their commanders. It was a bitter irony that the crisis period of the Battle of Moscow should see Hitler treat their achievements almost as if they did not deserve remembrance. And it was equally ironic that he did this with complete justification.

WINTER ORDEAL: THE PURGE OF THE GENERALS

The first clear-cut defeat suffered by the German Army since the outbreak of the war occurred on 30 November 1941 when a Russian counterattack flung Kleist's Panzers out of Rostov and forced the most easterly units of Army Group South to pull back. Rundstedt put it to Hitler that Army Group South must withdraw to the line of the Mius river and dig in there for the winter. Hitler refused. Rundstedt protested, was overruled, sacked, and replaced by Reichenau. He was only the first of many such scapegoats. After the Russian offensive began only one order was forthcoming from Hitler: 'stand fast'. He remained impervious to all pleadings that such an unyielding line could only result in hideous casualties.

Assaulted by heavy Russian forces at Kerch, Graf von Sponeck, the veteran of Rotterdam, withdrew his 47th Division. For this he was court-martialled on Hitler's orders and sentenced to death. The death sentence was commuted to life imprisonment but Sponeck did not survive the war: he was liquidated by the SS in March 1945.

Other generals quitted the scene in rapid succession. Not all were out-of-hand dismissals, for the strain of 'Barbarossa' had taken its toll on many. Brauchitsch was one of them; he had had a bad heart attack in November and was quite worn out.

He was replaced by Hitler himself, who coolly took over as the new Commander-in-Chief of the Army, although Halder stayed on as Chief-of-Staff. Bock, too, was exhausted and asked to be relieved. He was relieved as commander of Army Group Centre by Kluge but was soon hauled back into service, for Reichenau died suddenly in January 1942. Leeb had also asked to be relieved, which meant that when Küchler took over from Leeb, Bock was the only experienced army group leader left.

Kluge's accession to the command of Army Group Centre precipitated many changes. General Gotthard Heinrici replaced Kluge in command of 4th Army. Strauss was sacked from 9th Army and was replaced by General Walther Model, soon to be nicknamed 'the Führer's fireman' for his energy and skill in restoring hopeless-looking situations. Model rapidly proved his capabilities and was a key man in shoring up the front of Army Group Centre during the winter battles. Hoeppner was sacked as well, also for withdrawing his forces without permission. Hoth took over from Höppner. Not even ace commanders like Guderian were immune. After a long series of violent arguments with Hitler about the impossibility of maintaining position in the conditions at the front, Guderian was dismissed and replaced by General Rudolf Schmidt.

The appalling conditions of the winter battle in Russia and the nightmare way in which the fresh new Siberian divisions seemed impervious to them paralysed OKW as well as the wretched fighting troops. Even Keitel was treated to constant contemptuous tongue-lashing by Hitler, who now emerged in a startling new light. Moscow and the winter campaign was his great moment. His often-quoted remark to Jodl that 'This little matter of operational command is something that anyone can do' is unfortunate because it gives the impression of unbalanced flippancy. But it is now accepted that Hitler's 'stand fast' order, however ruthlessly enforced and however many thousands of men it condemned to death and mutilation, saved the Wehrmacht during that first terrible winter of 1941-2. By taking over direct control of the Army and by weeding out every single general who showed signs of wavering, Hitler prevented its wholesale massacre. Time would prove that this was his greatest achievement.

It would also prove that it had fatal results on the conduct of subsequent operations.

AFRICAN TRIUMPH

As the summer of 1941 approached, Rommel's natural obsession was with Tobruk, where the Australian garrison was still holding out. But at Tobruk it became apparent that Rommel's flair for mobile warfare had a serious blind spot. Throughout late April and May he continued to batter obstinately away at the western sector of the Tobruk perimeter, suffering losses he could ill afford. He had not made an adequate reconnaissance of the perimeter before attacking but had charged head-on at the nearest sector he came to. It was a serious mistake which he was to make again in the future.

At OKH there was grave dissatisfaction with Rommel's unorthodox and unauthorized carryings-on. The main worry was supply, and Rommel's attitude to supply was 'that's your problem'. Here was another blind spot. Given the speed with which Rommel had seen the possibilities of mobile warfare and the skill with which he exploited the unfamiliar terrain of Libya, it must be admitted that he did not want to know about where his petrol, food, ammunition, reinforcements, tank replacements, etc. were coming from until too late. In short, in North Africa the top generals had to be their own quartermasters. None of them could fight as they liked without having first arranged their supply-lines. Halder tried hard to bring Rommel to heel, sending out his deputy, General Friedrich von

Paulus, to assess the situation before Tobruk and report back. Paulus's reaction was predictable : the troops before Tobruk were having to put up with far too much and their supply-lines were not up to it. Not that anything concrete came of Paulus's visit ; however, 15th Panzer Division finally arrived, giving Rommel a more encouraging proportion of German troops.

These first attacks on Tobruk convinced him of one thing : the uselessness of Italian troops. Never a man of tact when he saw that something was wrong and tried to put it to rights, Rommel caused grave offence by his outspokenness on the subject. To a large extent this was unfair. Italian tanks, for one thing, were mechanized travesties compared to the battle-tried Panzer Mk. IIIs and IVs wielded by the Germans.

Rommel's aims in this early summer of 1941 were twofold : to maintain the investment of Tobruk and to strengthen his positions on the eastern frontier in order to ward off any relief attempts which the British might care to try. He saw to it that the most intelligent use was made of the natural features of the passes on the frontier, digging-in 88mm AA guns for use in an anti-tank rôle and ensuring that the mobile units were kept in reserve to strike when the main effort of any British push had been identified. In June these precautions paid off handsomely when Wavell's abortive Operation 'Battleaxe' came lumbering across the frontier. Rommel's gunners hammered the slow Matildas and brand-new, unreliable Crusader tanks as they headed up to the attack. Once the direction of the British advance was clear Rommel sent his Panzers into action, hooking repeatedly at the flanks of the British columns as they fell back in confusion. 'Battleaxe' was one of the best victories ever won by Rommel. Here was the virtuoso of the improvized advance showing that he could handle a calculated defensive battle with the right degree of coolness. It seemed that he had learned the lessons taught by his lack of patience before Tobruk.

Between June and November the desert war consisted of one long lull. It was the period of the big build-up for an autumn showdown. On the British side Auchinleck replaced Wavell and was working on the creation of a new army – the 8th – out of the original, diminutive 'Western Desert Force' which had chased the Italians out of Libya in December 1940–January 1941. The 8th Army's début would be a carefully-planned, large-scale offensive into Libya to relieve Tobruk and, if all went well, smash right through to Tripoli. It was also during this period that Auchinleck felt himself obliged to issue one of the most significant general orders of the day, making it clear to his subordinate commanders that far too much stress was being put on the idea of 'Rommel' instead of 'the enemy'. Poor Auchinleck had a thankless job. The man who was most culpable in this respect was Churchill himself, who became genuinely obsessed with the bogeyman image of the desert virtuoso. 'Rommel, Rommel, Rommel, Rommel', he was once heard to explode, 'Whatever matters but beating him ?'

The Rommel legend had been born and the British were the chief midwives. Goebbels's propaganda machine was strangely slow to hail the heartening new chain of victories over the British in North Africa. Rommel himself was indifferent. When he did react to the press coverage he was getting in the Reich it was usually in anger or contempt at the mendacity or extravagant statements made by the press hacks. If the British, from the lowliest patrol returning after rough handling by Afrika Korps units, to Churchill himself, were obsessed with Rommel's aura, he himself was obsessed with one objective : the capture of Tobruk. To this aim he worked steadily through the summer and early autumn of 1941, preparing for a new attack which would hit the weakest sector of the fortress perimeter. By complete coincidence the dates selected by Auchinleck and Rommel for their respective offensives were almost identical : 18 November for 'Crusader', the British attack, and 20 November for Rommel's attack on Tobruk. So it was that Rommel's plans were anticipated by those of Auchinleck, but this did not matter much. The German-Italian forces massing for the attack on Tobruk were in exactly the right place to block a relief attempt from Egypt, with the mobile force of the Afrika Korps poised to counter-attack from the open desert.

By November Rommel's command had been up-graded in status. He was now commander of the *Panzergruppe Afrika,* and his key subordinate was General Cruewell, commander of the Afrika Korps. Here a word of explanation is necessary as the phrase 'Afrika Korps' is more often than not misused. The 'Afrika Korps' meant the 15th Panzer Division and the 21st Panzer Division (as the 5th Light Division had been re-christened), the purely German, armoured core of Rommel's bi-national command. In November 1941 it was commanded by General Ludwig Cruewell, a wily and shrewd Panzer com-mander of Rommel's own stamp. The establishment of *Panzergruppe Afrika* had provided Rommel with an approp-riate staff, but he never made proper use of it. The lure of the front line was always too much for him. When he happened to be at the right place at the right time, this meant that he could personally order a move that could transform the battle. But as often as not his separation from his staff had critical results. Both happened in the Crusader battles of November-December 1941.

'Battleaxe' had been a personal triumph for Rommel; 'Crusader' was an out-and-out defeat for which he was to blame. He started well, with the two divisions of Afrika Korps taking full advantage of the inept way in which the British chose to scatter their armour all over the desert as they advanced to the relief of Tobruk. Devastating counter-attacks completely disrupted the British attack and forced Auchinleck to intervene personally, sacking General Cunningham of 8th Army and replacing him with General Ritchie, in order to keep up the tempo. But then Rommel threw it all away. Instead of keeping his forces neatly concentrated and continuing to grind down 8th Army, he took off into the blue on his famous 'dash to the wire' (the wire being the barbed-wire entanglements originally put up by the Italians along the frontier). His aim was to throw the 8th Army's rear areas into panic and provoke a retreat. It would be cited today as a typical piece of Rommel brilliance if it had come off – but it failed. Instead the New Zealand Division kept going and relieved Tobruk – the object of the exercise. Rommel came racing back and managed for a while to cut off Tobruk once more, but his armoured units had been whittled down so much that he could no longer continue to

They could have stopped the Nazi 'revolution' at birth: Fritsch, Blomberg, and Raeder.

Field manoeuvres with the Führer: Blomberg at left, Fritsch at centre. Within months both would be ignominiously ousted from their posts.

He tried to incite the General staff to resign rather than go to war over
Czechoslovakia; resigned himself; became a key conspirator against
Hitler; and died after the failure of the 'July Plot': Ludwig Beck.

Brauchitsch, successor to Fritsch—frequently reduced to the verge of a nervous breakdown by Hitler's outbursts.

Ceremonial turn-out for a state visit by Hungarian Regent Admiral Horthy. Hitler and Ribbentrop stand apart, eyed by Raeder and Brauchitsch.

Comparatively unknown shot of Hitler visiting a field kitchen in Poland. The officer on his right is Rommel, then commander of the Führer's personal bodyguard.

Camaraderie on campaign. Episodes like this caused immense difficulties; the German propagandists were eager to show the Führer sharing the food of the troops—but he was a confirmed vegetarian, necessitating frantic stage-management.

OKW versus OKH. Hitler and 'lackey' Keitel confer with a sour-looking
Halder and Army C-in-C Brauchitsch.

Rundstedt, one of the hard-core Wehrmacht professionals, veteran of Poland, France, and Russia—who had the ironic duty of pronouncing Rommel's funeral oration.

Rommel, shown here in the days when he could do no wrong in Hitler's eyes—and before he became convinced that the Führer was leading Germany to ruin.

Glory days. The 'Desert Fox' in his element.

Hitler with the ever-present Keitel, Bock, and Guderian.

Kesselring, defender of the Italian front, who
made a mockery of Churchill's 'soft underbelly'
thesis.

Situation conference. Second from left is Paulus, before he received the field appointment which led him to disaster at Stalingrad.

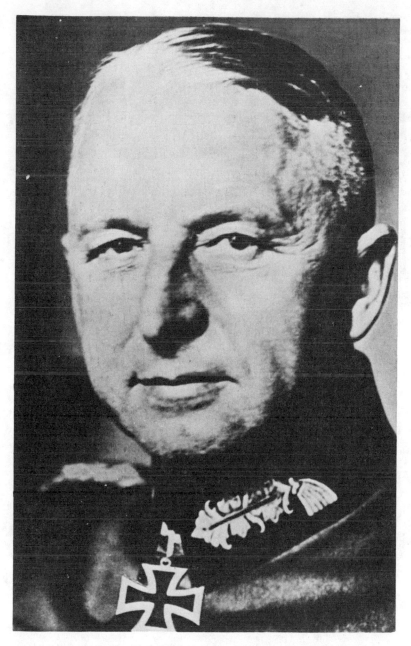

Manstein, conqueror of Sebastopol—and the master-mind behind the great German recovery after Stalingrad.

Hitler, Guderian, and Fegelein (Eva Braun's brother-in-law). Guderian's holograph dedication reads: 'In memory of joint effort in the service of our Führer.'

fight a battle of attrition. He made the sensible decision to cut his losses and pull back to El Agheila to build up the *Panzergruppe* for another day. His overall performance in the 'Crusader' fighting has prompted the interesting thought that he was never really happy with an army-sized command, but was another man once his forces had been ground down to divisional size. Certainly his withdrawal of the battered *Panzergruppe* was a masterly one which dealt out many a bloody nose to 8th Army as it moved up in pursuit.

What happened next stood the course of the desert war upside-down and was the result of a combination of factors. The first was the basic rule of the North African campaign, namely, that as one army advanced it got further and further away from its main base while the opposition fell back on its own. When 8th Army's advance units closed up on Rommel's position at El Agheila towards the end of December they were in much the same breathless condition that O'Connor's had been the year before. And the second factor was that a consignment of tanks got through to North Africa just at the right moment, on 5 January, thus doubling the armoured strength of the *Panzergruppe*. Added to that was the fact that once again the British were forced to pull troops out of the desert theatre, for Japan was now in the war and reinforcements were desperately needed in the far east. Rommel seized his chance with both hands and attacked, again without telling his superiors what he was up to. His first attack went in on 21 January 1942. By the end of the first week in February he had bundled 8th Army back to the 'Gazala Line', a chain of minefields and desert strongpoints blocking the direct approach to Tobruk between Ain el Gazala and Bir Hakeim. Once again, for the moment, it was stalemate.

Both sides set about building up their forces for a renewed offensive – but this time the 8th Army were beaten to it. Rommel's *Panzerarmee Afrika* (it had received yet another up-grading since 'Crusader') attacked on 26 May. Rommel's brief was clear. He was granted permission to launch another offensive and, if possible, take Tobruk. After this he was to halt while Malta was captured, thus blowing the keystone out of the

British blockade of the central Mediterranean and ensuring an
uninterrupted flow of Axis supplies to North Africa. Then, and
only then, he could prepare for a further offensive to invade
Egypt and take the Suez Canal. By this time, too, Field-Marshal
Kesselring had been appointed Commander-in-Chief, South,
charged with gaining control of the air in the central Mediterranean and acting as a glorified spokesman and quartermaster
for the *Panzerarmee*. He and Rommel were both in full agreement that Malta must be taken. But they differed widely over
the priorities. With his first-hand knowledge of the difficulties
of getting anything like enough supplies through to North
Africa, Kesselring was only prepared to countenance operations which could be adequately supplied. But with his
instinctive feel for when, to use Napoleon's phrase, 'the battle
was ripe', Rommel was not prepared to let anyone call him off
from the pursuit of a beaten enemy.

And that in essence was what happened after the tremendous
Battle of Gazala in May–June 1942, which culminated in the
achievement of Rommel's long-cherished dream : the capture
of Tobruk. Tactically speaking this battle was Rommel's
masterpiece ; it was extremely hard-fought and he came very
close to defeat until his supply-lines were punched through the
Gazala Line to revive the hard-pressed Afrika Korps. Again,
to be fair, he was helped to a considerable extent by the piecemeal tactics of the British, who squandered their considerable
advantage in armour by launching penny-packet attacks which
did little but immolate themselves against the German anti-tank
guns. Once he had levered 8th Army out of its position along
the Gazala Line, Rommel immediately regrouped for an attack
on Tobruk, which he hurled in at the precise spot where he had
planned to attack the previous November. Breaking in on 20
June, Rommel's forces soon managed to overturn the disorganized British defences and he received the surrender of the
fortress on the following day. His career had reached its zenith ;
the capture of Tobruk earned him his field-marshal's baton
from a delighted Hitler. But he was immediately faced with the
cruel dilemma of whether or not to allow the 8th Army to get
away while the Axis forces in the Mediterranean took Malta,

or to keep it on the run and try to chase it clean out of Egypt.

He chose the latter, appealing direct to Hitler and Mussolini over Kesselring's head. Although a mistaken move – Rommel himself admitted that the dash into Egypt was a 'try-on' – it is not hard to see why Hitler backed this sudden chance for a dazzling strategic success where previously he had only seen an annoying sideshow. The pursuit itself was carried out at the same pace as the advance of 7th Panzer in France in 1940, with the added hardship of the heat of the African summer. And it ended at Alamein in the first days of July when Rommel repeated the same error which had kept him out of Tobruk in April–May 1941. He attacked the first defences he came to, laying himself wide open to counter-attack and enabling Auchinleck to fight him to a standstill. Foiled at Alamein, the *Panzerarmee* dug in, frozen at high tide, at the end of the longest line of communications it had ever had, and anticipating a new build-up period for future victories that were not to be.

DRIVE TO STALINGRAD

The ordeal of the winter battles of 1941-2 on the Eastern Front had made it clear even to Hitler that there could be no question of a general resumption of the offensive by all three army groups in summer 1942. With the coming of spring, plans were being laid for a concentrated punch by Army Group South which was nevertheless intended to win the war.

First, there was to be a direct advance east to the Volga, capturing Stalingrad and holding it as a firm pivot. Originally Hitler hoped that if sufficiently punishing losses could be inflicted on the Red Army, the Wehrmacht would then be able to wheel northwards up the Volga and cut in on Moscow from the east. But gradually – as had happened during the height of the 'Barbarossa' advance in the previous summer – Hitler's original plan to push home the main attack on the northern flank faded. Instead he began to talk in grandiose terms of the conquest of the Caucasus and the Kuban, with the great south Russian oilfields which, he asserted, once secured, would win the war for Germany.

But the great German offensive of summer 1942 was preceded by two fierce battles, the first in the Crimea and the second in the Ukraine, where the Red Army made a determined bid to recapture Kharkov. In the Crimea Manstein, who had been promoted to the command of 11th Army the previous autumn, earned his baton by overrunning the peninsula and capturing the fortress of Sebastopol. And in the Ukraine the Russian thrust against Kharkov was cut off and smashed by energetic counter-attacks from north and south. Kleist's 1st Panzer Army (all the original *Panzergruppen* had been upgraded in status by the time of the Battle of Moscow) formed the southern claw ; the northern claw was 6th Army, now under the command of Paulus. A capable staff officer who had acquired the courtier's knack of keeping his ear to the ground and impressing people in the right places, Paulus was earmarked for high office in the OKW. Now he was being given the chance to show what he could do in the field.

Although Army Group South was to carry the weight of the 1942 offensive, it was divided into two subordinate Army Groups : 'A' (List) and 'B' (Weichs). In Hitler's plan Army Group 'A', which included Kleist's 1st Panzer Army, would push south and take the oil-bearing region, subsequently extending to the whole of the line of the Caucasus. 'B', including Hoth's 4th Panzer Army, would handle the crossing of the Don and the capture of Stalingrad. It was, to start with, a sound and feasible programme which promised dire results for the Russians. But after a brilliant beginning it was thrown into jeopardy by the intervention.

When the offensive began on 28 June 1942, Bock was still in overall command of Army Group South. He followed his brief well, holding back Paulus's 6th Army to clear the Don at Voronezh while Hoth's 4th Panzer Army headed straight for Stalingrad. He was right to do this, for it soon became apparent that the Red Army was not going to fall into the trap of the previous summer and lose hundreds of thousands of men in useless encirclement battles. But then Hitler took a hand. Reviling Bock for 'wasting time' by over-caution at Voronezh, he sacked him. Army Groups 'A' and 'B' were given independence of action. And – key error – Hoth was ordered to suspend his drive on Stalingrad. Instead he was to head south and help Kleist get across the lower Don.

This, as Kleist was not slow to point out, was not only totally unnecessary but positively obstructive. The two Panzer armies arrived on the Don almost simultaneously and the congestion on the roads and bridges was acute. Kleist crossed the Don between 25 and 27 July ; Hoth did not get across until the twenty-ninth – only to find that new orders had been drawn up for him. The 4th Panzer Army, having been sent looping off to the southward, was now to wheel to the north-east and attack Stalingrad from the south.

In his south-easterly advance towards Stalingrad, Paulus had not been having things all his own way. By the end of July he had decided to halt on the Don and wait for Hoth to come up from the south before moving against Stalingrad in strength. By 19 July all was ready and the two armies moved forwards to drive the two defending Russian armies – 62nd and 64th, both decisively outnumbered in armour and manpower and definitely the worse for wear – into the Volga. Within three days the left-wing corps of 6th Army – Wietersheim's XIV Panzer Corps – had struggled through to the northern suburbs of Stalingrad and was overlooking the Volga. On the night of 23-4 August General Wolfram Freiherr von Richtofen's IV *Fliegerkorps* set the city ablaze from end to end with mass incendiary raids. But still the Soviet armies did not break. Hoth was stopped in his tracks at Tundotovo, south of the city ; 6th Army was left with Wietersheim's narrow corridor through the northern suburbs. The last week of August crept by with no improvement in the situation and by the thirty-first it was obvious that a set-piece attack would have to be made if the city was to be cleared of its obstinate defenders.

At the beginning of the campaign Stalingrad had only been envisaged as a blocking point, a strategic base from which decisive advances were to be made, but it was about to adopt a new and totally different role. This was contrary to every military principle followed by the Wehrmacht since the out-break of war : a killing-ground for a trial of strength, a battle-field where the watchword was attrition – the Verdun of the Eastern Front.

Part III
DEFEAT

'LONG LIVE THE 6th ARMY!'

In Poland, in Belgium, in Russia during the first months of 'Barbarossa', even as late as the Kharkov offensive of May 1942, the generals had proved their skill at reaping the most advantage from faulty enemy moves and dispositions. But at Stalingrad they were hoist by their own petard. The dull-witted Paulus continued to batter his way forward into the city at a cost which any Allied general would have found familiar on the Western Front in the First World War. And across the Volga Zhukov was planning to convert the crisis at Stalingrad into a decisive breakthrough. He deliberately kept the battered divisions of 62nd Army just strong enough to hold out, feeding in sufficient reinforcements to keep the battle going until his preparations were ripe.

Paulus can be excused for not guessing what Zhukov was up to until it was too late. But there can be no excuse for his failure to polish off 62nd Army in double-quick time.

First, he had the strength. The 6th Army was the spearhead of the 1942 offensive, extra-strong in infantry, armour, and artillery, and it had the air support of an entire *Fliegerkorps*. Second, he may not have been a seasoned campaigner himself but his officers and men were ; and the head-on, broad front attacks he made them carry out threw away their chances of victory. What he should have done was to have the Luftwaffe concentrate on knocking out the Russian ferries across the Volga and neutralizing the Red Army artillery on the far bank. With his ground forces, he should have concentrated his attacks north and south of the city, working them inwards towards one another in such a way as to roll up the tenuous strip of ground still held by the Russians. The initial advances on Stalingrad by Wietersheim and Hoth had put 6th Army into an admirable position for the employment of these attacks – but Paulus did not use them, and for that he alone was responsible.

Paulus compounded his ignorance by sacking his two Panzer corps commanders, Wietersheim and Schwedler, for protesting that it was madness to keep tanks stuck up at the forward edge of a stationary front where all they could do was get knocked out by shellfire. It was also at this time that another miniature purge of the generals occurred. Down in the Kuban, Kleist was running out of steam as the 1st Panzer Army approached the Caucasus. His forces had taken the oilfield at Maikop (although the Russians had fired it before the Panzers arrived) but could not reach Grozny, the other key oil town. Kleist's superior, List, was made scapegoat and was dismissed by Hitler. In fact, Jodl nearly went, together with List. Hitler had sent Jodl down to List's HQ to express the Führer's displeasure at Army Group 'A's tardiness. When Jodl returned with the news that List had done all that a man could do to carry out his orders Hitler exploded with rage, ordering the dismissal not only of List but of Jodl. However he soon rescinded the latter order and Jodl stayed on. He had learned one lesson well: not to give Hitler bad news at the wrong time. Jodl did not make that mistake again.

September 1942 also saw the fall of Halder. Since Hitler had taken over from Brauchitsch this had only been a matter of time, for the two jarred more and more on each other the more they had to work together. Hitler's pretext for sacking Halder was nothing to do with the situation at Stalingrad. It came about as the result of a silly disagreement over the timing of a possible Soviet offensive against Army Group Centre. Halder went. Hitler replaced him as Chief-of-Staff with General Kurt Zeitzler.

By the beginning of November even Paulus had begun to detect signs of the Russian build-up, but its size was grossly under-estimated. Half of this was the wish being father to the thought, for Paulus was preparing for one last effort to clear the remnants of 62nd Army right out of Stalingrad. This last offensive began on 11 November and soon went the way of its predecessors, petering out into a mêlée of vicious hand-to-hand engagements. It was still grinding miserably on when, on 18 November, Zhukov's counter-offensive began. Within four days massive Russian pincers had met at Kalach, the bridgehead over the Don over which all the supplies of 6th Army had to pass. Paulus and his men were cut off in Stalingrad.

To start with, things were bad but by no means desperate. A prompt disengagement and breakout would have saved 6th Army and almost certainly restored the front. In one way Hitler and Zeitzler did react promptly, sending down Manstein to form a new 'Army Group Don' and restore the situation. This was on 20 November, before the Kalach bridge was lost. But Manstein did not arrive until the twenty-fourth, having had to travel by train, and by then Hitler had already ordered Paulus to stay put. Even if Hitler had authorized a breakout it would hardly have been possible for 6th Army to have redeployed in under five days. But once again Göring's vanity intervened. To ingratiate himself with Hitler he assured the Führer that the Luftwaffe could keep 6th Army supplied by airlift. Zeitzler desperately tried to get Hitler to accept that this was a flat impossibility, quoting the totals of supplies which 6th Army would need daily and the totals which the Luftwaffe could actually deliver. All he got, however, were repeated airy assurances that the Luftwaffe could do the job. Even though Zeitzler lost his temper and called Göring a liar to his face, Hitler refused to listen to reason. Statistics always tended to lose their magic for him when they spelled out unpleasant facts.

What was worse, Paulus believed it too, and this deprived him of any sense of urgency in making up his mind about a breakout. Manstein had got clearance for an emergency relief operation, 'Winter Storm', to coincide with a breakout ('Thunderclap') by 6th Army. By 12 December he could wait no longer and Hoth's 4th Panzer Army launched 'Winter Storm'. After ten days of desperate fighting Hoth's tanks had battled their way to within twenty-two miles of the Stalingrad pocket but could do no more. Hoth was forced to retreat before heavy Russian attacks. The 6th Army was doomed.

The whole episode is without doubt the one episode in the war when the way in which Hitler and his generals worked hit rock bottom. Manstein and Zeitzler were pressing for the breakout. Paulus shilly-shallied, egged on by his Chief-of-Staff, General Artur Schmidt, who echoed the theme that 6th Army would still be in position by Easter if it were properly supplied. In addition Paulus claimed that he did not have enough fuel to break out, anyway, and when Manstein went back to Hitler in desperation Hitler pointed out that Paulus did not have enough fuel ... it was a ludicrous tangle of crossed wires, and it strangled 6th Army.

The last act began on 9 January 1943 with massive concentric attacks against the Stalingrad pocket, which was now surrounded by seven armies. It ended in the first forty-eight hours of February, when 6th Army, forced back into the frozen ruins of Stalingrad, was split into two pockets and surrendered. Hours before, Hitler had promoted Paulus to field-marshal in order to give the tragedy a Wagnerian touch, for no German field-marshal had ever been taken prisoner. Paulus was not of Wagnerian stamp, however – as Hitler complained viciously when he heard of the surrender.

Not only Paulus but sixteen divisional, corps and staff generals and the wreckage of twenty divisions were removed from the board in the Stalingrad disaster. In Berlin Goebbels and his copy-writers set to work to sanctify the destruction of 6th Army as Germany went into four days of national mourning: 'The 6th Army is not dead. The 6th Army will never die. Long live the 6th Army !'

It seemed an irreparable loss. But within weeks Manstein's genius transformed the situation and completely restored the Eastern Front.

MANSTEIN'S MASTERPIECE

The last resistance in Stalingrad ended on 2 February 1943. In the next three weeks the runaway Soviet offensive continued until it seemed that nothing could stop the Red Army reaching the Dniepr and achieving an encirclement which would dwarf that at Stalingrad. But by the middle of March the Russian advance had been halted in its tracks, hurled back to the line of the Donets river, Kharkov had been recovered, and the entire situation had been reversed. For a battle of sheer importance it ranks with the 'miracle of the Marne', although to compare it with that accidental shambles is something of an insult. It was a brilliant piece of classic strategy, and it was the work of Manstein.

For months now, Manstein had come to believe that the only way in which the Wehrmacht could hope to hold its own in Russia was not to try and fight for every foot of ground whenever the Red Army unleashed one of its offensives. Only numerical parity would have made that possible and that was exactly what the Wehrmacht did not have. What the Germans did have was the experience and skills of their Panzer elite. What the Russians had was a stiff and rigid command system which tended to panic when hit by the unexpected. Manstein was therefore convinced that the way the Wehrmacht should fight on the Eastern Front was the 'back-hand' offensive:

deliberately allowing deep breakthroughs – the deeper the better – and then chewing them off with concentrated Panzer attacks and rolling up the Russian line.

And after Stalingrad he got his chance. What he achieved not only proved his theories to the hilt but will always rank among the most skilful battles ever fought.

His first victory was in persuading Hitler that the 'stand fast' order would be of no earthly use in the present situation. He had to put in a lot of hard talking before he made his point, but Hitler agreed to give him a free hand at a meeting on 6 February. For the next fortnight, as the Russian spearheads drove steadily closer to his headquarters, Manstein bided his time, neatly positioning the withdrawing armies – Kleist's 1st Panzer, Hoth's 4th Panzer, and three improvised 'Army Detachments' named after their commanders, Hollidt, Kempf, and Fretter Pico – where they would be best situated for the counterstroke. Then, on 22 February, he struck.

Manstein's spearhead was the 4th Panzer Army, consisting of XLVIII Panzer Corps with three Panzer divisions and the Waffen SS Panzer Corps, consisting of the *Leibstandarte* and *Das Reich* divisions. Led with the greatest energy, these concentrated armoured thrusts sliced off the probing Russian tentacles at right-angles, driving on to recover Kharkov and the line of the Donets and once more restoring a firm, eastward-facing front to the Wehrmacht in Russia. Unfortunately the *rasputitsa* – the Russian 'rainy season' when the terrain dissolves in mud – intervened before Manstein could round off his victory by reducing the westward-bulging salient between Orel and Belgorod. He was certainly not helped by the unwillingness of Kluge to cooperate with attacks by Army Group Centre, and so the attack on the salient was shelved. Manstein hoped that the problem could be taken up no later than the end of April, before the Red Army had time to make the salient too tough a nut to crack.

Despite the brilliance of the Manstein counterstroke of February–March 1943, it seemed likely that some time must pass before the Wehrmacht could renew the offensive on the Eastern Front. On 20 February Hitler had made his peace with

Guderian, who had been cooling his heels in virtual retirement since his dismissal in December 1941, with the words, 'I need you'. Guderian was offered the post of Inspector-General of Armoured Troops, with the task of overhauling the Panzer arm. It was high time that German tank manufacture and supply was licked into shape, and that proper scope was given for the formidable new Tiger and Panther tanks. But the honeymoon period did not last long. Guderian was unable to get Hitler to see that with new weapons sufficient time must be granted to iron out the bugs before committing them in battle.

And the Panthers would not be available in quantity until July, when the Russians would have had three months to fortify the Kursk salient . . . .

ALAMEIN TO 'TUNISGRAD'

When Auchinleck fought the exhausted *Panzerarmee* to a halt at Alamein in early July 1942 the real hollowness of Rommel's situation became apparent. Even assuming that he could make good his tank losses with repairs and whatever replacements could be got through from Italy, they would be so much scrap iron without fuel. And so between 'First Alamein' in July and 'Second Alamein' in October – when Montgomery attacked – Rommel's relationships with Kesselring were based on non-stop reproaches that Kesselring was not delivering the goods as promised. At last, bitterly, Rommel was forced to accept that the dash into Egypt before the reduction of Malta had been a cardinal error.

Throughout August, however, he was husbanding the resources of the *Panzerarmee* for another attempt to break through the Alamein Line before the British made it too strong. He knew that this was a do-or-die effort, for if it failed he could do nothing but stand on the defensive. With the 1942 Russian campaign still in full swing the last things he could count on were troop reinforcements. But Rommel was about to find out the hard way that a lot had changed in the desert since the first heady victories of the Afrika Korps.

The first was air supremacy, which had now passed irrevocably to the British. The second was Churchill's replacement of

Auchinleck with Alexander, and the appointment of Montgomery to the command of 8th Army. Montgomery made it clear that under his leadership nothing would be taken for granted apart from the way the Germans had always won *their* battles in the past desert campaigns. From now on the *Panzerarmee* would be tackled with its own tactics : keeping the armour concentrated, making use of anti-tank weapons to the full, with the strongest units where they should be at the right time. And then there was manpower and *materiel,* in which Montgomery held all the cards. The tough new Sherman tanks were on their way to the desert, a match for the best Panzers in the desert. At last, after three years of campaigning in North Africa, the British were about to get a proper tank.

Rommel's final breakthrough attempt was launched on the night of 30 and 31 August. It was largely a repeat of the Gazala plan – a swinging hook round the southern flank of 8th Army – and it was not hard to forecast. Suffering heavy losses in the perimeter minefields, the Afrika Korps struggled eastwards and prepared to attack the core of the 8th Army's position : the Alam Halfa ridge. Montgomery was waiting for him, however. The Afrika Korps was pounded by non-stop bombing and intense artillery fire and Rommel was forced to call off the attack. He would have had to do so in any case because of the shortage of fuel, and as it was he had to wait until nightfall on 2 September before beginning the withdrawal. It had been a costly experiment : fifty tanks were left on the battlefield, while Montgomery had not even had to mount one large-scale armoured counter-attack. From then on the *Panzerarmee,* as Rommel had feared, was on the defensive at Alamein.

Gone were the days when Rommel was prepared to leave the supply problem to others while he got on with the fighting. He was caught with a vengeance now, for without adequate fuel – 'more petrol' was his major demand in the weeks before 'Second Alamein' – he would not be able to fight another long-drawn battle, let alone retreat. And so he set about making the front of the *Panzerarmee* as nearly impregnable as he could, ordering the sowing of 445,000 mines. With his armour carefully deployed in order to provide immediate local counter-attacks wherever the British broke through, he hoped to delay the offensive, when it came, for as long as possible.

However, when Montgomery's massive bombardment crashed out on the night of 22 October, Rommel was not in North Africa. He was at a mountain resort near Vienna, where he had been packed off on doctor's orders, suffering from liver and blood-pressure trouble. *En route* to his retreat he had had several empty interviews with Hitler in which he was promised *Nebelwerfer* rocket mortars with which to boost the *Panzer-armee*'s fire power, and forty Tiger tanks and new self-propelled guns. Rommel also had the trying chore of holding press interviews, in which he had to do his level best to appear confident as to the outcome of the coming ordeal in Africa. Meanwhile the final preparations on the Italo-German front were left to Rommel's deputy, General Georg Stumme – by coincidence, the officer from whom he had taken over command of 7th Panzer Division back in 1940.

Stumme, poor man, did not last long. He was motoring up to the front line to assess the situation for himself at dawn on 24 October when a burst of fire fell near his vehicle. It seems that Stumme had a heart attack and fell from the car; his body was later recovered. For the first twenty-four hours of the crucial test of strength at Alamein, the *Panzerarmee* was leader-less. When Rommel arrived at the front he knew at once that his armour, thanks to the fuel shortage, would not have the necessary mobility to combat the scale of Montgomery's offensive. Nevertheless the 'dog-fight' at Alamein lasted over eleven days, with the *Panzerarmee* giving of its best. By the morning of 2 November, however, Rommel and General von Thoma, current commander of the Afrika Korps, knew that the game was up. And on the third, to add insult to injury, he received a drum-beating telegram from Hitler which concluded with the incredible statement: 'It would not be the first time in history that a strong will has triumphed over the bigger battalions. As to your troops, you can show them no other road than that to victory or death.'

4 November was the day when the long retreat began. Rommel would never have been able to get away with it had

8th Army been poised to clinch its victory by trapping the disorganized units of the *Panzerarmee*. On 5 November the *Panzerarmee* was back at Fuka, on 7 November at Matruh. And on 8 November he received the appalling news that strong Anglo-American forces had landed in Morocco and Algeria. Now there could be no hope of another stand at El Agheila, the western gateway to Cyrenaica. He must retreat right through Tripolitania to Tunisia.

Kesselring's reaction to the Allied landings in North Africa (Operation 'Torch') had been lightning fast. He had rushed German troops into Tunisia to hold Tunis and Bizerta and establish a front as far to the west as possible. Thus when Rommel's *Panzerarmee Afrika* reached the Tunisian border on 13 February it found that General von Arnim's 5th Panzer Army had stabilized the Tunisian front. Rommel would have to hold the frontier defences of the Mareth Line against Montgomery's 8th Army while Arnim coped with the Anglo-American 1st Army. Rommel, however, rose to the situation with a flash of his former audacity. He proposed a joint attack by the Afrika Korps and Arnim's 10th Panzer Division against 1st Army which would cut it in two and, given a healthy slice of luck, push through to the Mediterranean coast and create an African Dunkirk.

The result was the Battle of Kasserine, launched on 14 February, which scored rapid initial successes against the green American troops in the Allied line but which was eventually ground to a halt. By 22 February Rommel and Arnim had scored nothing more than a hefty dent in the Allied front and a withdrawal was essential.

One more battle remained for Rommel in Africa. This was a pre-emptive strike against 8th Army, again with the Afrika Korps and 10th Panzer Division, at Medenine. It was a fiasco. The Panzers ran straight into devastating anti-tank fire and suffered heavily – the British had, in fact, been expecting the attack for days. Shortly after the repulse at Medenine Rommel, still a desperately sick man, left Africa for ever – and Armin took over command of 'Army Group Africa'

Army Group Africa ! Here was a far cry from the days when

a junior commander had chased the British out of Cyrenaica with little more than one under-strength Panzer division. Too late, the Axis had realized the vital importance of maintaining a foot-hold in North Africa. The Allied pressure was steadily maintained, and Arnim's army group was pushed back into Tunisia proper. When the final break-through came in May 1943, a quarter of a million German and Italian troops surrendered. Coming so closely after the Stalingrad débâcle, it was inevitable that the surrender in Africa should be tagged by many as 'Tunisgrad'.

Kesselring had proved his worth as a *Luftflotte* commander and as a 'political general', like Eisenhower, coordinating the conflicting interests of two allies. Now, charged with the defence of Sicily and southern Italy, he was to prove himself one of the most versatile land commanders Germany produced in the Second World War.

KESSELRING'S SOUTHERN FRONT

The battle for Sicily lasted from 10 July 1943 to 17 August, when the last Axis troops were evacuated. In this struggle Kesselring had again to move fast, putting in his XIV Panzer Corps under General Hube to shore up the crumbling Italian defences. Hube's two divisions could do little but delay the Anglo-American conquest of the island, with the 'Hermann Göring' Panzer Division and the 1st Parachute Division particularly distinguishing themselves. For Kesselring the real test came when Mussolini was deposed and Italy surrendered – the immediate prelude to the Allied landings in southern Italy.

It was an amazing performance. Kesselring had to cope simultaneously with the occupation of central and southern Italy, the disarming of local Italian forces, and the containment of the Allied forces which landed in Calabria and the Gulf of Salerno. Not only did he accomplish all this : he overcame fears at OKW that the Italian surrender must mean the Allied occupation of all Italy south of the Apennines. Hence the establishment as early as 26 August of Army Group 'B' in the Po valley, under Rommel. Rommel, in fact, viewed the whole Italian situation with an extremely pessimistic eye and believed that it would be quite impossible to hold the Allies in southern Italy. Kesselring believed that it was essential to do so. As a Luftwaffe general he was only too keenly aware of the

importance of keeping the advanced Allied air bases as far to
the south as possible ; and he was confident that unless the
Allies aimed a concentrated punch directly at Rome he would
be able to hold the narrowest part of the Italian 'boot' as a firm
front.

Thus he had to play an extremely testing guessing-game as
to where the main Allied landings would come. He put General
Richard Heidrich's 1st Parachute Division down in Calabria
to act as a blocking force. General Herr's LXXVI Panzer
Corps covered Rome. And the Gulf of Salerno, which
Kesselring regarded as the obvious landing area for a move
against Naples, was covered by 16th Panzer Division.

As a result he was able to withdraw slowly in the face of
Montgomery's slow advance up from the 'toe' of Italy while
16th Panzer nearly brought off a 'Dunkirk' against the British
and American forces which landed at Salerno on 9 September.
Once he had marked down the Salerno landings as the main
Allied effort, Kesselring threw in the 'Hermann Göring'
Division and the 9th Panzer Grenadier Division as fast as he
could, although the speed of this redeployment meant that these
divisions were not able to fall upon the Allied beach-head as
concentrated units. Nevertheless the situation at Salerno
remained very serious for the Allies until 82nd Airborne
Division was dropped into the beach-head in the early hours
of the fourteenth. Mass bombing attacks hammered the
German positions, and the Allies were also able to use the
15-inch broadsides of the elderly battleships *Warspite* and
Valiant to add to their fire-power.

Kesselring's chances of victory at Salerno depended on
whether or not the German divisions actually containing the
beach-head could eliminate it before Montgomery's 8th Army
fought its way up from the south. He kept up the tempo for as
long as he possibly could, but when the last heavy German
counter-attack was held and broken up by bombing and shellfire on the seventeenth he decided that the time had come to
call it a day. A week before, on the tenth, Kesselring and the
commander of the German 10th Army, General von Vietinghoff, had agreed on the next line of defence which must be held

if southern Italy had to be abandoned. After the nine-day battle of Salerno, Kesselring therefore set in motion a planned withdrawal to the Cassino Line, where he proposed to stand and fight it out again.

This first phase of the campaign in Italy had been dictated by Kesselring's sensitivity on the subject of air power, by his determination to deny the Allies every possible air base he could. It was a principle with which OKW should have been thoroughly sympathetic because the lightning German advances of the past had always depended on moving the Luftwaffe's advanced bases as far forward as possible. Kesselring's strategy in southern Italy should also have appealed to Hitler, who always stressed the vital importance of shielding the Rumanian oilfield at Ploesti from Allied air attacks. Instead of intervening and giving Kesselring every possible division in Italy to keep the Allies off the airfields of the south, Hitler vacillated between Kesselring and Rommel until 21 November, when he appointed Kesselring supreme commander of Army Group 'C' – of the Italian theatre, in short – and transferred Rommel to France to superintend the completion of the 'Atlantic Wall' defences. With the latest setbacks in Russia to worry about, OKW's failure to concentrate on Italy was hardly surprising. But it meant that Kesselring had to carry on by himself, without any assistance from his superiors, during the vital opening weeks of the campaign when the Allied forces were still dispersed and at their most vulnerable.

Naples fell to the Allies on 1 October; and the rest of the month was taken up with their painful advance through the atrocious conditions of an unusually foul Italian autumn. Clark's sights were set on Rome; Montgomery's on Pescara and Ancona. But none of these objectives was to be attained until the summer of the following year. General Hube's XIV Panzer Corps blocked Clark; General Herr's LXXVI Panzer Corps blocked Montgomery. Heidrich and 1st Parachute Division acted virtually independently during the retreat from Apulia. There was fierce fighting for the Volturno and Sangro rivers – for the Allies, in these miserable weeks, it seemed an eternity of 'one more river to cross' – but by the middle of

December, 5th and 8th Armies had managed to close up to the hard-core German defences across the narrow 'waist' of Italy. And there they stuck.

The month of October also saw one of the most heartening achievements made by the Wehrmaht in the whole war. When it became clear that Monte Cassino had been selected as a focal point of Kesselring's new defence line, one man was extremely troubled. He was Colonel Julius Schlegel, a staff officer in the 'Hermann Göring' Division, an art lover whose first thoughts were for the priceless treasures of religious art and documents in the magnificent library of Monte Cassino abbey. After several attempts he managed to convince Bishop Gregorio Diamare that the Abbey and its treasures were living on borrowed time, and the Bishop gave Schlegel permission to arrange the transfer of the Abbey's treasures to the Vatican in Rome. This Schlegel accomplished on his own initiative – but while the transfer was still in full swing the Allies broadcast that 'the Hermann Göring division was plundering the Abbey'. Prompt enquiries were ordered by Kesselring, but Schlegel managed to convince Kesselring's representatives and his own divisional commander, Conrath, of the truth of the matter and the work went on. On 3 November it was completed, and the Bishop and Monks of the Abbey contemplated the future in the knowledge that the embodied tradition of the Benedictine order was safe in Rome whatever might happen at Monte Cassino.

Between 9 November and 28 December the 8th Army made another attempt to break through to Pescara on the Adriatic front. Montgomery was brought to a halt by two factors: his own 'set-piece' method of attack, which created masses of rubble to block the advance of his own tanks ; and the tenacity of Heidrich's paratroop units, which it proved impossible to break. And the direct approaches to Cassino itself – and the Liri valley, the gateway to Rome and Clark's main objective – were covered by General Frido von Senger und Etterlin's XIV Panzer Corps.

Von Senger's 29th Panzer Grenadier Division (General Fries) and the 44th Infantry Division *Hoch und Deutschmeister*

('The High and Mighties') had their work cut out between 2 December 1943 and 15 January 1944, in which time the Allies battered their way forward to the very threshold of the Cassino defences. It had taken them two and a half months to penetrate what the Germans called the 'Reinhard Line', an outer screen intended to slow up the Allied advance for as long as possible ; and in that two and a half months the total Allied advance was a mere twelve miles. But despite the magnificent defence put up by the defenders of Cassino the long-term strategic plan formulated by Field-Marshal Alexander was beginning to work. This was to force the Germans on to the horns of a dilemma in which they would be too heavily engaged to pull out of Italy even if Kesselring wanted to, and forced at the same time to send to Italy divisions which would otherwise be used to challenge the Allied invasion of France. What the Allied attacks in December-January achieved was to force Kesselring, Vietinghoff, and von Senger to fling every available unit into the line at Cassino. Meanwhile an amphibious landing well behind the German front was in preparation, timed to coincide with the January attacks at Cassino, which must result in a breakthrough.

But it did not. The landings at Anzio and Nettuno on the morning of 22 January came as a complete surprise to Kesselring ; it was some six hours before they were spotted by a passing Messerschmitt. But Anzio did not, as the Allies expected, force Kesselring to denude the German front at Cassino. Instead he vamped up an entirely new front which took full advantage of the Allied caution in advancing inland and which managed to seal off the forces at Anzio. He turned the Anzio front over to General von Mackensen's 14th Army Headquarters, brought down from northern Italy.

So it was that by mid-February 1944 the German position in Italy was as follows. At the end of December Kesselring's front was 85 miles long. Anzio extended it to 120 miles. He had to throw in four extra divisions, and his monthly losses were such that he was being sent on average 15,000 replacements which, when evened out, came to something like one division per month. Thanks to his shifts and improvizations, which more than cancelled out the advantages in surprise which the Allies had been able to gain, he was still holding fast well to the south of Rome, instead of trying to hold between Pisa and Rimini, which had seemed most likely when the Italians had surrendered seven months before. Thanks to the magnificent fighting qualities of his troops and the energy of his subordinates – Hube, Heidrich, and von Senger foremost among them – Kesselring had achieved the seemingly impossible despite the tardiness and doubts at OKW and the strong cards held by the Allies.

A splendid achievement indeed – but one which was doomed to be undermined by the disastrous course of events on the Eastern Front and the growing concern with the reinforcement of occupied France.

RUSSIAN STEAMROLLER: FROM KURSK TO THE DNIEPR

Taking the performance of Hitler and his generals at Stalingrad as depressing in the extreme, the story of the offensive at Kursk in July 1943, and its disastrous aftermath, is even worse. Misapprehension, personal rivalry, and rank stupidity all combined to create a crushing defeat, to squander all the advantages gained so painfully in preceding months, and to turn the tide on the Eastern Front once and for all.

It will be recalled that Manstein had always regarded an offensive against the Kursk salient as an essential completion of the task begun with his counter-offensives of February and March. The spring thaw had intervened just at the wrong moment. Like every other front-line commander he was completely aware of the Russian genius for rapid build-ups which cancelled local weaknesses within weeks. The longer the attack was postponed the longer the odds against a German victory became. Yet *Zitadelle* – 'Citadel', code-name for the Kursk salient offensive – was postponed almost as many times as *Fall Gelb* had been during the winter of 1939-40. And this time the reasons were far more complicated.

Hitler was naturally reluctant to admit that the Wehrmacht had yielded the initiative by ordering it to stand on the defensive throughout 1943. He wanted to attack and the Kursk salient was the obvious place – but he also wanted to attack with the new Panther tanks which were being rushed into service under the combined urgings of *Reichsminister* Albert Speer and Inspector of Armoured Forces Guderian – and it was clear that the Panthers would not be ready in time for an attack in April or May. In fact it was not until 10 May that Hitler was told that 324 Panthers would be available by 31 May – which meant that *Zitadelle* could not be launched until mid-June at the earliest. And this in turn meant that the Russians in the salient would have been given over two months in which to get ready.

Guderian therefore joined Manstein in urging that *Zitadelle* be abandoned, as it amounted to a total and unnecessary gamble. First, it would mean the commitment of the entire German armoured reserve built up since Stalingrad. Second, it would mean inevitable heavy losses. Third, there was no guarantee of a decisive victory, even assuming that the salient could be reduced. Fourth – the most worrying of all – another Soviet breakthrough in anything like the strength which had bitten off 6th Army in the previous November, would meet no mobile counter-move whatsoever.

Guderian found an unexpected ally in Jodl, who was looking at the war on all fronts and was not liking what he saw. The writing was on the wall in the Mediterranean and whatever the Italians chose to do it was obvious that a 'southern front' must at some time be created and maintained. Then there was the question of the cross-Channel invasion. It was not surprising that the Chief-of-Staff of OKW opposed the squandering of priceless reserves, with worries such as these in mind. But Jodl's viewpoint was largely cancelled by that of his boss, Keitel, back in favour again and determined to stay there, who parrotted Hitler's assertions that the Wehrmacht must launch a summer offensive in Russia 'for political reasons'.

And for once the heads of OKW and OKH were in agreement, for Zeitzler, too, was backing *Zitadelle*, Zeitzler had made an auspicious début as Army Chief-of-Staff at the time of the closing of the Stalingrad pocket, urging an immediate breakout and calling Göring a liar for asserting that 6th Army could be supplied by air. But by May 1943 he was locked in a private feud of his own with Jodl, whose influence over Army matters Zeitzler strongly resented. Zeitzler's reasons for attacking at Kursk were fallacious in the extreme. He accepted that as far as reserves were concerned the Wehrmacht did not have much to play with. But he asserted that it was for that very reason that the Wehrmacht must attack – and attack where the Red Army concentrations were strongest – in order to upset the Soviet preparations for a fresh offensive.

Another leading personality also had a personal axe to grind and he, too, backed *Zitadelle:* Kluge, whose Army Group Centre had played second fiddle ever since the winter offensive of 1941-2. His former feud with Guderian – who apparently had lost by being dismissed in December 1941, but who was now restored to favour with increased powers – had flared up again. Kluge continued to snub Guderian and be generally offensive. It was mutual, and Guderian made no bones about how he felt. The outcome, however, was too much even for Hitler : Kluge challenged Guderian to a duel and invited Hitler to be his second ! What a gift for Allied propaganda this would have been (not to mention the Allied war effort) – the commander of Army Group Centre and the Inspector-General of Armoured Forces squaring up to each other with pistols. Hitler ordered both parties to make it up, and Guderian added a parting dig by writing an apologetic letter to Kluge in which he apologized for any offence caused, but stated that his feelings towards Kluge were the result of the injustice done him in December 1941 which had yet to be righted.

On 3 May a tentative date was set for *Zitadelle:* 13 June. A week later Hitler was given the tank production figures drawn up by Guderian and Speer. It was after this conference that Guderian besought Hitler to give up the idea of *Zitadelle* : what was the offensive *for* ? Hitler admitted that the idea of *Zitadelle* 'made his stomach turn over', but added that he was as yet undecided. This was true. By the beginning of June the Panzer production figures had all been met, but reports from the front told ominous tales of the formidable defences prepared by the Russians. Hitler therefore decided to wait until three weeks' more tank production had joined the front – thus giving the Russians three weeks in which to make those defences still more formidable. 'D-Day' for *Zitadelle* was fixed at last : 4 July.

It would be a joint effort by Army Groups Centre (Kluge) and South (Manstein). Model's 9th Army would attack from the northern flank of the salient ; the veteran Hoth, with 4th Panzer Army, would strike from the south. Hoth carried the main punch, with nine Panzer divisions including the SS Panzer Corps with *Totenkopf, Leibstandarte,* and *Das Reich,* with three infantry corps covering his flanks. Model's 9th Army had nine Panzer divisions and two supporting corps. It was the greatest concentration of armour ever assembled for a single German offensive – but it had been made at the cost of stripping practically every army on the front of its armoured support.

The OKW, in short, had made the very mistake which had doomed Gamelin's armies during the Western campaign of 1940 : no strategic reserve.

Within hours of the beginning of the offensive the splendid new tanks were in trouble. The density of the Russian anti-tank guns had been vastly under-estimated and the Soviet commanders had been canny in concealing their positions. Thanks to the respite granted by the spring thaw and Hitler's postponements of the attack, the Red Army forces in the salient had built up a defence system eight belts deep, with the emphasis put on anti-tank work : mines and guns. By the morning of the sixth it was obvious to the Panzer commanders that things had gone terribly wrong. Despite all the classic Blitzkrieg preparations for a sweeping breakthrough, the battlefield of the Kursk salient had congealed into a positional warfare in which the Russians held all the cards. Model came off worse ; on his front the Panzer units had been issued with the massive new *Elefant* assault guns – Tiger hulls with limited-traverse 88-mm guns but no machine-guns for close-in work against enemy infantry. This made the *Elefants* sitting ducks for the Russian infantry, which they could not hurt. The infantry, on the other hand, could get in close and knock them out with well-aimed flame-thrower bursts. Down on the southern sector Guderian's warnings about the teething troubles of the Panther tank were also coming home to roost. 'They were easily set ablaze,' noted the chief-of-staff of XLVIII Panzer Corps; 'the oil and petrol systems were inadequately protected and the crews were inefficiently trained.'

After five days of intense fighting two small dents had been hammered into the shoulders of the Kursk salient but it was clear that a decisive breakthrough had not been achieved. Total ground gained consisted of about nine miles – a pitiful showing compared with the epic breakthroughs of the past. And on the twelfth the concentrated survivors of 4th Panzer Army met in a head-on, eight-hour clash with the armour of the Soviet 5th Army – an epic tank battle with nearly 3,000 tanks of both sides involved overall. Already the northerly thrust of Hoth's Panzer divisions – which still had sixty-odd miles to go before they could join up with Model – was being dissipated in westerly attacks to secure the flanks of the limited penetration actually achieved.

The attacks were resumed by the weary Panzer units on the fourteenth, but time had already run out for *Zitadelle*. Hitler summoned Manstein and Kluge on the fifteenth and laid it on the line: the attack on the salient must be called off at once. The first news had come in of the Allied landings in Sicily, and Hitler was determined to cope with this new threat by weeding troops out of the Eastern Front. All forces must be pulled back. Manstein argued in vain that it was too late, that it would be extremely dangerous to disengage – let alone weaken the front – while the Red Army was poised to take the offensive itself; but Hitler was adamant. He had had his way; he had sent his revitalized Panzer force into premature battle and had seen it mauled beyond repair. With the first attacks on the Kursk salient the Wehrmacht had sown the wind; now it was to reap the whirlwind.

The first reaping had begun even before Hitler called off *Zitadelle*, when the Russians counter-attacked in the Orel salient, north of Kursk. Model's 9th Army, its strength already enfeebled by its heavy losses against the northern face of the salient, was now assaulted in flank and threatened with annihilation. Obsessed with his plan to withdraw as many troops from the front as possible, Hitler – for once – gave his permission for withdrawal, and by 5 August Orel had been abandoned. Now Kluge got all the action he wanted as subsequent Soviet offensives flamed northwards along the front like a powder-train, hustling Army Group Centre and forcing it back towards Smolensk.

South of the salient, however, Hitler's orders were the same as usual : no withdrawal. He was going to hang on to as much of the Ukraine for as long as possible, which was unfortunate because it was the hardest part of the Eastern Front to defend. This did not prevent OKW from hauling the SS Panzer Corps out of the line and earmarking it for the Italian theatre. On 3 August the inevitable happened and the Red Army rolled forward south of the salient, its sights set on the destruction of Army Group South.

As soon as it started Manstein knew at once what had to be done. After *Zitadelle* there could be no question of the dazzling armoured counter-strokes which had restored the German front after Stalingrad. On 8 August he told Zeitzler that Army Group South must either pull right out of the Donets bend or be reinforced by another ten divisions from Army Groups Centre and North. Naturally this was turned down and Manstein resigned himself to the loss of Kharkov – this time for good – which fell on 25 August. Desperate work by 4th Panzer Army fought the Russians to a halt outside Poltava by the end of the month, but it was only a respite. Further to the south two more Russian army groups got across the Donets and the Mius rivers and drove west towards the Dniepr, threatening the sealing-off of 11th Army in the Crimea. Manstein was forced to do the only thing he could : order a 'scorched earth' policy into operation and pull Army Group South back to the line of the Dniepr. September was a month of constant retreat, seeing the Red Army liberate Bryansk and Smolensk and close up to the river on the heels of the retreating Wehrmacht.

The fierce fighting of the autumn and winter of 1943-4 saw the Wehrmacht forced back into the last corner of the western Ukraine, to the line of the Carpathians, and through the Baltic states to the outer approaches to the Reich itself. Hoth, Kleist, and eventually Manstein himself were dismissed, Model taking over from Manstein as the new commander of Army Group South. Also in these gloomy months, Guderian made repeated efforts to drum up support which would relieve Hitler of his personal comand of the Army. In his search for a backer in high places he even went to see Goebbels, who received him extremely politely but remained noncommittal. A final attempt to win over Jodl in November was equally unsuccessful.

'Can you think of a better supreme commander than Adolf Hitler ?' Jodl asked acidly.

ROMMEL IN NORMANDY

In November 1943, while the Allied push towards Rome was grinding to a halt before the outer defences of the Monte Cassino Line, and while the German defences along the Dneipr were beginning to crumble, Hitler suddenly gave Rommel a new appointment. He was relieved of his empty post as C-in-C, Army Group 'B' in the Po valley and sent to France as inspector of the coastal defences between the Pyrenees and Denmark: Hitler's much-vaunted 'Atlantic Wall'. And it was there that he immediately began to put into practice all the lessons he had learned since his dash through France with 7th Panzer Division in 1940 – lessons which had one single aim. That aim was the defeat of the cross-Channel Allied invasion, whenever it might come.

After his first tour of the Atlantic defences Rommel roughed out his initial ideas in a report to Hitler, dated 31 December. In essence, these ideas never changed. They bear the stamp of his impotence at Alamein throughout. The enemy must not be allowed to break out of the coastal defences. He would be most vulnerable before his troops could actually get to grips with the defenders: in other words, before the first landing-craft grounded. Mines, mines, and more mines – dense minefields covering every foot of the coast – would be the best weapon in the German armoury. They would have the additional advantage in that the heavily-mined coastal strips could be handed over to reserve or auxiliary units, releasing the best troops for service elsewhere. Much heavier fire-power was essential : machine-guns and anti-tank guns for hacking down enemy infantry and tanks as they came floundering up the beach.

To keep the number of landing-craft that did hit the beaches down to a minimum, submerged obstacles along the foreshore must be quadrupled. Rommel envisaged four concentric belts of obstacles, set to cover every phase of the tide. These varied from simple stakes with mines on the end to elaborate, concrete and cast-iron structures which would disembowel any landing-craft unlucky enough to hit one. Inland from the beaches all possible landing-sites must be sown with anti-landing devices to foil enemy airborne forces, both paratroop and air-landed.

It was an inspired appointment which is certainly worth marking up to Hitler's credit : Rommel was made for the job. His natural energy and genius for improvization had been proven in Africa : they would both be needed now as never before. Moreover, since Tobruk in the high summer of 1942 it must be remembered that Rommel's career had been one long frustration. Now he was out on his own, the man whose work would defeat the invasion, and he rose magnificently to the challenge.

Hindsight, alas, has proved that Rommel's appointment came too late – too late, that is, to defeat an invasion in June 1944. In three years on the Atlantic coast the Wehrmacht had achieved appallingly little. Much of this was due to the fact that all the top generals had been needed in other theatres, and that those other theatres had always had top priority for man-power and *materiel*. When Rommel was appointed to make the 'Atlantic Wall' a reality, the Commander-in-Chief, West, was Rundstedt, who was old, tired, and cynical about the whole business. He was certainly not the man to throw himself into the task. But Rommel was.

From the very first day of his appointment Rommel toured the entire sector under his command, dropping in on lonely coastal batteries, supervising working parties, chatting to the troops and generally putting the fear of God into all and

sundry. So little had been done! He had estimated that for the
French coast alone, twenty million mines would be needed to
create the defensive zones he had in mind as essential. When
he took over only 1,700,000 mines had been laid *in three years,*
and only 40,000 of them were being delivered per month.
Press-ganging French factories and Army ordnance depots into
mine production, Rommel had got four million more mines
laid by the time of D-Day and – if given time – he had his
sights set between fifty and a hundred million.

With Rundstedt as his immediate superior, Rommel worked
under immense difficulties. He himself commanded Army
Group 'B' which had 7th Army in Brittany and Normandy,
15th Army in the Pas de Calais, and 88th Corps in Holland.
The south of France was entrusted to Army Group 'G' under
General Blaskowitz, who had played a very unexciting role
since he had received the surrender of Warsaw in 1939.
Blaskowitz was responsible for the Biscay coast (1st Army) and
the Mediterranean coast (19th Army). It was obvious that
Rommel's army group would be the one which would take the
shock of the invasion, but he did not have the authority to
control the Luftwaffe units in his territory ; and the big coastal
gun emplacements were the preserve of the Navy ; Rommel
could do little or nothing to control their siting. Hitler had also
intervened to make a thorough nonsense of the control of the
armour in the sector of Army Group 'B'. Rommel was left with
direct control over the 2nd, 21st, and 116th Panzer Divisions,
but as from 26 April Hitler laid it down that the other Panzer
divisions – Panzer *Lehr,* 1st SS, and 22nd SS, would be hus-
banded in 'OKW reserve', under Hitler's own hand. Thus
Rommel would be unable to order the one thing he knew would
be essential as soon as the principal Allied landing had been
marked down: a decisive armoured counter-stroke which
would throw the invaders back to the beaches and smash them
there. This decision was largely influenced by inspection tours
carried out by Jodl and his deputy, Warlimont, and by the
commanding general of 'Panzer Group West', General Geyr
von Schweppenburg – a man who had never had the bitter
experience, as Rommel had in Africa, of knowing what it was

like trying to command large armoured forces when the enemy retained complete command of the air.

Ironically enough – as had happened when Montgomery launched his Alamein offensive in October 1942 – Rommel was not on the spot when the Allies landed on 6 June 1944. He had set off for Germany to visit his family and to see Hitler, encouraged by meteorological reports that no invasion would be possible for the next fortnight. There was additional irony in the fact that the invasion came just at the moment when it really looked that he would be able, as he had first opined back as early as January, to beat off the attack. Alerted by his extremely able Chief-of-Staff, General Hans Speidel, early on the sixth, Rommel came rushing back from Germany, to find to his despair that the Allied air forces had had no trouble in securing total air supremacy over Normandy and that the 'free' Panzer divisions had not been rushed to the beaches. One solitary Panzer raid – a battle group from 21st Panzer – had indeed carved through to the coast and caused much alarm and despondency before it was forced back. The memory of this raid, which bore out all Rommel's previous ideas on how the armour should be used in Normandy, was a particularly bitter one.

Enough had been done, however, to keep the British out of Caen (which Montgomery had marked down as the final objective for D-Day) and a fierce series of battles for the town began. With his vast numerical superiority, however, Montgomery could afford to make it a battle of attrition. He was able to do more, and by keeping up the pressure on the Caen sector, draw the bulk of Rommel's armour there like iron filings to a magnet, weakening the German left flank and eventually contributing to the decisive Allied breakout on 25 July.

Before that date, however, much had happened to the German command in the West. On 29 June Rundstedt and Rommel saw Hitler at Berchtesgaden. It was an uncompromising visit: they were trying to convince him that the game was up in Normandy. Rommel had come to see, as Guderian had done long ago, that plain talking was the only way with Hitler.

On the seventeenth, at a meeting with Hitler near Soissons, Rommel had bitterly complained at the massacre of the French civilians at Oradour-sur-Glane by the SS *Das Reich* Division and had demanded that *Das Reich* be punished for the atrocity. Rundstedt, too, had had enough. At Berchtesgaden on the twenty-ninth, when Keitel intercepted him, bleating, 'What shall we do ? What shall we do ?' Rundstedt snapped : 'Make peace, you fools ! What else can you do ?' Keitel immediately went to Hitler with the story and Rundstedt was dismissed. The new broom as Commander-in-Chief West was the man who had just seen Army Group Centre torn to shreds by the Russian 1944 summer offensive : Kluge.

As far as Rommel was concerned, Kluge started well and truly on the wrong foot by breezing into Rommel's HQ on 5 July, reeking of optimism that jarred hideously on the jaded western commanders, and telling Rommel in the presence of two staff officers that now he, Rommel, would have to get used to taking orders. Rommel, incensed, complained to Kluge in writing, adding a list of the arguments which he had put forward since D-Day, and blaming the split German command for many of the failures which had occurred. To be fair, Kluge, though at times a thoroughly unpleasant man (his blood feud with Guderian should also be remembered) recognized harsh reality when he saw it, and soon realized that Rommel had been in the right.

Kluge, however, did not work with Rommel for long. After a ten-day interlude in which the German commanders desperately strove to shore up the buckling front around Caen, Rommel was knocked out of the battle by enemy action. Travelling back from Panzer Group West HQ on 17 July his car was spotted and pounced on by one of the swarming British fighters. Rommel was badly wounded in the head in the crash and was rushed to hospital.

Kluge therefore had to tackle the Allied breakout on his own. But it is another commentary on that complex man that on the twenty-first Kluge sent Hitler a copy of Rommel's latest situation appreciation in which he endorsed every word that Rommel had said about the campaign. Not that it made much difference. Hitler found it no more difficult to order his generals to stand fast in France than in Russia.

But the endurance of the German forces penning the Allies in the Normandy beach-head had been reached.

THE BOMB PLOT AND AFTER

Five days before General Patton's tanks smashed their way out of the Normandy beach-head, an event took place at OKW headquarters in East Prussia for which many generals had been secretly longing since the Sudeten crisis of 1938 and before. A bomb exploded in the room in which Hitler and his staff were stooping over a situation map, shattering the room 'with the impact of a 150-mm shell'; and for several confused hours it really seemed that the incredible had happened and that Hitler was dead.

The fact that it took so long to find out that Hitler was very much alive was typical of every single conspiracy to depose the Führer, let alone take his life. It is a chronicle of ineptitude blended with bad luck – and one which underwrites the murkier side of the characters of Hitler's generals. The last serious involvement of high-ranking Army officers in the anti-Hitler conspiracy had been in autumn 1939, when Brauchitsch and Halder had backed down, asserting that it would be wrong to provoke a state crisis while the enemies of the Reich were still in the field. But after 'Barbarossa' began in June 1941 the Army conspiracy began to take shape again; and it was organized by idealistic staff officers in the Army unit destined for immortality in German history by taking Moscow : Bock's Army Group Centre.

The staff officers principally involved were Henning von Treskow and Fabian von Schlabrendorff, working in active collaboration with Admiral Canaris, the head of Armed Forces Intelligence (*Abwehr*) and his Chief-of-Staff, Colonel Oster. Tresckow and Schlabrendorff conceived the plan of kidnapping Hitler on a visit to the front and calling him to account ; and they began to sound out all the top generals they could lay their hands on, including their own C-in-C Bock, and Brauchitsch. As before, however, they got absolutely no firm commitments from any of their superiors and were forced to shelve their plans for several months.

Matters were very different, however, after the shock of Stalingrad, and during the lull before *Zitadelle* another plot took shape. This was 'Flash', a much more ambitious plan for an Army coup which would not leave matters solely in the hands of the plotters at the front. Confederates in the Reich itself would act simultaneously to win over the Army garrisons in Berlin and other key cities. Key man in Berlin was General Friedrich Olbricht, deputy of General Friedrich Fromm, who commanded the Replacement Army. Olbricht and Tresckow hoped to win over the commander of Army Group Centre, Kluge, and Tresckow had a potent weapon ready to hand : moral bribery. He had seen a letter from Hitler to Kluge referring to a hefty cheque for some £20,000 which had been paid to Kluge for services rendered – other accounts have it that Tresckow saw the actual cheque. Certainly Tresckow was in a good position to put Kluge's conscience on the rack, but that was all he achieved. Kluge turned down a daring plan to have Hitler gunned down on a visit to Army Group Centre HQ ; and Tresckow and Schlabrendorff fell back on the idea of planting a bomb on Hitler's plane and liquidating the Führer in a mid-air explosion – which would have the additional merit of being attributable to an accident.

Tresckow got the bomb aboard Hitler's plane on 13 March 1943, disguised as two heavily wrapped bottles of brandy as a present for General Helmuth Stieff at OKH. The bomb was set, handed over, taken aboard, and the plane took off – but two hours later came the crushing news that Hitler's plane had

landed safely. Schlabrendorff, with incredible daring, flew to
OKW the following day to retrieve the 'brandy bottles' after
Tresckow had telephoned to say there had been a mix-up in the
packages – praying to God that the bearer, Colonel Brandt,
had not unwrapped the package in the meantime.
Schlabrendorff's courage was rewarded. He handed over two
genuine brandy bottles, took a train to Berlin, and investigated.
The time mechanism had functioned perfectly, but the
detonator was defective.

Next came a series of suicidal attempts on Hitler's life, in
which volunteer heroes proposed to stand next to Hitler with
time bombs in their pockets and blow themselves and the
Führer to pieces. All these attempts were foiled, however, by
Hitler's constantly changing his timetable and either leaving
early or not turning up where the conspirators were waiting for
him. And then, in December 1943, the first attempt was made
to leave a bomb in Hitler's HQ by the most remarkable
character the German resistance movement produced.

He was Colonel Klaus Schenk von Stauffenberg, a member
of Olbricht's staff, an extremely able staff officer who had
recently recovered from severe wounds received on active
service in Tunisia. Standing in for Olbricht, Stauffenberg tried
to leave a briefcase-bomb in Hitler's conference room on 26
December, but was foiled by the meeting being cancelled. A
cultured and sensitive man, Stauffenberg was determined that
Hitler must be eliminated and he was by no means disconcerted
by this initial failure : he intended to try again. He set to work
to enlist new help from the Army via his chief, Olbricht. Beck
he already knew, and respected, but he wanted an active field-
marshal as well. Witzleben had been pencilled in as Armed
Forces Commander-in-Chief after the coup succeeded, but
Stauffenberg well knew the immense value of enlisting a more
prominent figure. Kluge still refused to commit himself. So did
Manstein. And then, in February 1944, came startling news
from France. Rommel himself was willing to back the
conspirators.

Rommel was first sounded out by General Heinrich von
Stülpnagel, Military Governor of France, and General

Alexander von Falkenhausen, Military Governor of Belgium. But Rommel was eventually persuaded to commit himself by an old civilian friend – who also knew Goerdeler well. This was Dr Karl Stroelin, Mayor of Stuttgart, who persuaded Rommel that he was the only man who could avert civil war in Germany. Rommel had long believed that Hitler had to go but he was against killing him – it would make the Führer a martyr-figure. The Field-Marshal was prodded further down the path of conspiracy by his chief-of-staff, Speidel, who arranged a meeting between Rommel and Stülpnagel on 15 May 1944, to rough out the basic premises for the coup. Rommel was too open a character not to have another try at bringing in Rundstedt, who had already demurred on the grounds that to overthrow Hitler would infringe the oath of loyalty taken ten years before. But Rundstedt's attitude was : 'I leave it to you.'

The hopes of the Western generals in the plot were painfully naïve. Once Hitler was disposed of – and tried by a German court – they would negotiate for an end to the war in the West. No unconditional surrender. Europe was to remain united under the German aegis, apart from the restoration of France, Belgium and Holland. Most of them really hoped that the British and Americans, on the conclusion of such a peace, would be only too glad to join Germany in the fight against Soviet Russia. D-Day and the start of the battle for Normandy only reinforced their view that Hitler must be disposed of as quickly as possible.

Stauffenberg and the Berlin planners had meanwhile evolved 'Valkyrie', the plot to take over the military centres in the Reich once Hitler was dead. Ironically enough Hitler knew all about 'Valkyrie' : it had originally been dreamed up as an emergency measure to put down any insurrection by the millions of foreign workers in the Reich. Now 'Valkyrie' was to be the cover for the conspirators' takeover attempt. There was one serious snag. The only officer who could give the executive order for 'Valkyrie' was the evasive Fromm, but plans had been laid to arrest him and replace him with Höppner, former *Panzergruppe* commander until his disgrace in 1941.

Then, on 17 July, came the stunning news that Rommel, due

to his injuries in France was out of the running. The most
prestigious figurehead in the conspiracy would not be available.
To Stauffenberg this new setback made no difference. He was
determined to assassinate Hitler whatever happened.

Three days later he duly made his attempt. He placed his
briefcase-bomb six feet away from Hitler and left the conference room, pleading an urgent telephone call from Berlin.
There he waited a tense five minutes before seeing the conference room go up with a deafening explosion. Confident that
nothing could have lived through it, he bluffed his way out
through the Rastenburg perimeter gates and sped back to the
airport to return to Berlin.

What had saved Hitler? First, the conference was not being
held in a concrete bunker but in a wooden hut with the win-
dows open, which dissipated the blast considerably. This need
not have mattered and in fact several men in the room were
killed. What was crucial was that Colonel Brandt – the very
Brandt to whom Tresckow had entrusted the 'brandy bottles'
in March 1943 – had knocked his foot against the briefcase
and had shoved it further under the map table to get it out of
the way. This, plus the fact that Hitler was leaning over the
heavy table-top when the bomb went off, saved the Führer's
life.

While Stauffenberg was flying back to Berlin, exultant at the
thought that Hitler was dead and that his colleagues in Berlin
must be proceeding according to plan, the whole conspiracy
had begun to go terribly wrong.

Even though Hitler had survived, 'Valkyrie' could have
worked. Stauffenberg had enlisted the aid of General Erich
Fellgiebel, signals officer at OKW, whose task was to notify
Berlin that the attempt had been successful and then see to it
that OKW remained cut off from the world for the next three
hours. This he did. But the conspirators in Berlin – Olbricht,
Witzleben, and Beck – did nothing. Not until three hours later,
when Stauffenberg was back in Berlin, did 'Valkyrie' get under
way and by then it was too late. Fromm refused to cooperate
and the conspirators had arrested him, but the wires were
already humming from Rastenburg. The SS in Berlin sur-

rounded the War Ministry block in the Bendlerstrasse ; Fromm sentenced Olbricht, Stauffenberg, and other associates to death by shooting; Beck committed suicide; Höppner was arrested. That night Hitler broadcast to the German people and the last glimmers of hope were dead. The 'generals' plot' had been a total failure.

Hitler's vengeance was terrible. A wave of arrests and trials before the 'People's Court' began, with almost automatic sentences of death by hanging – the hanging, on Hitler's personal orders, being done from meat-hooks on nooses of piano wire. The trials continued well into 1945 – the Gestapo arrests totalled some 7,000. But not all perished on the meat-hooks. Tresckow went out into No-Man's-Land on the Eastern Front and killed himself with a grenade. Stülpnagel, ordered back to Germany, stopped his car and tried to shoot himself on the battlefield of Verdun, but only succeeded in blinding himself. He, too, was hauled before the People's Court and executed. But before he died he mentioned the name of Rommel.

Kluge, like Fromm, had refused to have anything more to do with the conspiracy on hearing that Hitler had survived, but suspicion soon fastened on him. The ten days after the failure of the plot saw the Western Front, in Kluge's own words, 'ripped open'; and on 17 August Hitler replaced Kluge with Model. The following day Kluge wrote a long farewell letter to Hitler, set off for Germany, and poisoned himself on the way.

Rommel's fate was the most calculated of all. Two OKW toadies, Generals Burgdorf and Maisl, came to his home at Herrlingen to escort him to Berlin. Once inside the door they gave him a deadly alternative : the People's Court, certain, ignominious death for himself and untold hardships for his wife and only son ; or a cyanide capsule, a tragic 'heart attack', a state funeral as befitting a hero of the Reich, and full provision for his family. He chose the latter, quietly told his wife and son that 'I shall be dead in a quarter of an hour', got into the car, and drove off. Within minutes the OKW generals solemnly reported Rommel's 'heart attack' by telephone. The state funeral was held in all its solemn magnificence, with Rundstedt pronouncing the funeral oration. Most sickening aspect of all were three gushing messages of sympathy from Hitler, Göring, and Goebbels. For one general the aftermath of the bomb plot brought rapid advancement: Guderian, abruptly summoned to Rastenburg and appointed Army Chief-of-Staff in replacement of Zeitzler on 21 July. Guderian soon found that his work was cut out, for after months of atrophy all was chaos at OKH. He was further hindered in his new duties (Hitler had not relieved him of his former post as Inspector-General) by the odious requirement of presiding over the new 'courts of honour', in company with Keitel, Jodl, and Rundstedt. These 'courts of honour' were held to decide whether or not implicated officers should be tried by the People's Court. If found guilty, the officer in question was discharged from the Armed Forces, stripped of all military privilege regardless of former rank, and handed over to the tender mercies of the People's Court.

This was only one of many humiliations forced on the Army. The right-arm 'German salute' became obligatory instead of the traditional military salute. Films of the executions were even shown in military academies such as Lichterfelde (where the nauseated cadets staged a walk-out as soon as the film started running).

How did the generals react to the news of the bomb plot? Virtually no general who backed it survived, let alone had the time to start writing about it. One is left with the reaction that more generals would have liked to have seen it succeed than admit the fact, although most standard memoirs convey a fair measure of the instinctive disgust felt by hard-case fighting men for subversive idealists – often to depressing lengths of self-righteousness.

DISASTER IN THE WEST

Having ruined his best chances of wrecking the Allied invasion by the chotic command set-up in the West; having ignored the warnings of the generals at the front ; having then ordered his forces in Normandy to put their heads in a trap and wait until it closed – Hitler sent Model to take over and win the day. Not surprisingly, he failed.

Patton's US 3rd Army launched its massive breakout attack – Operation 'Cobra' – on 25 July. By the thirty-first the racing American tanks had pushed south down the western side of the Cotentin peninsula and were poised to wheel eastwards to begin a vast encircling move that bade fair to trap every German division ordered to 'stand fast' by Hitler. Matters were made worse at the end of the first week in August by Kluge dutifully carrying out Hitler's order to counterattack through Mortain and cut the American break-out corridor – a counter-attack which had about as much chance of succeeding as the Franco-British counter-attacks against the 'Panzer corridor' in 1940. It was to be a three-division punch, using 2nd Panzer, 116th Panzer, and the SS *Leibstandarte* – but it never really got off the ground. The divisions found the greatest difficulty in moving up to their start-lines and the original timing of the attack went haywire. Mortain was captured on the seventh but the Allies hit back with non-stop air attacks that nailed the Panzers to the ground. On the eighth the American eastward wheel began – but Hitler ordered Kluge to attack again from Mortain. Kluge prepared to obey. He dared do nothing else, for the first 'People's Court' hearings had been opened in Berlin.

By the eleventh, however, Kluge's SS Panzer commanders, Hausser and Eberbach, were protesting loudly that the second Mortain counterattack was beyond the resources of their men. Hitler was notified by Kluge that the cautious, wait-and-see field marshal 'associated himself with their standpoint', which boiled down to pulling back from Mortain and blocking the American threat to Mortain. But Hitler insisted on retaining personal control of the battle in Normandy – from East Prussia! Getting a concrete decision out of Hitler under these conditions often took twenty-four hours – and then that decision would have been rendered a dead letter by the fast-moving events of this fluid phase of the campaign.

This was borne out by the forty-eight hours of 12-13 August, in which the Americans swirled forwards another thirty-five miles, taking Alençon and then swinging north towards Argentan, deep in the rear of the German divisions still under orders to attack westwards towards the sea, and only twenty miles from the Anglo-Canadian forces pushing southwards from Caen towards Falaise. This was the 'Falaise Gap', and any commander worth his salt would have ignored Hitler and ordered his forces to get out as fast as they could. But Kluge was thinking of himself now, not of his men. And on the fifteenth came the incident which proved his undoing. He completely vanished from the scene for over twelve hours, having been pinned down in a ditch by murderous Allied artillery fire and bombing attacks. Hitler seized on his absence as incontrovertible proof that Kluge was seeking to get through the Allied lines and either surrender himself or arrange for the capitulation of the entire Army Group. And on the sixteenth, as the crisis in the Falaise Gap rose to its height, Hitler summoned Model from the Eastern Front and packed him off to France to take over from Kluge.

By the evening of the seventeenth, when Kluge was replaced

by Model, the pocket was steadily being squeezed flat from three sides and its only exit was under constant air attack and artillery fire. Model took one look and did what should have been done days before : he ordered Hausser to pull out. The Allies managed to seal off the pocket twice in the face of desperate German attempts to break out ; as late as the twenty-first, II SS Panzer Corps was trying to cut through to the survivors in the pocket. But on that day Model accepted defeat and ordered a general retreat.

By this time Patton's spearheads were already across the Seine both east and west of Paris.

Model now made a strategic decision that ranks with Rommel's common-sense decision to retreat all the way back to Tunisia after he heard of the 'Torch' landings in Algeria. He knew that the German forces falling back on the Seine were a wreck, and that it would be touch and go whether he could get them across the river, let alone try and hold the far bank. By the twenty-ninth he managed to extricate large numbers across a bridgehead tenaciously held open at Elbeuf (where Rommel had failed to cross when heading in the opposite direction in 1940) – but the crossing, as the tough SS Panzer commander Sepp Dietrich admitted, was as disastrous as the Falaise Gap as far as equipment was concerned. In its first ten-week campaign on the new Western Front the Wehrmacht had lost half a million men in casualties – 210,000 of them prisoners of war. As far as the all-important armour was concerned it was an even bigger disaster than *Zitadelle* had been : nearly 2,200 tanks and assault guns lost west of the Seine.

Now, far too late, a new note was dominating the reports from the Western Front. Model did not submit his plans to Hitler for approval : he told him what he was doing. In this case it meant a headlong retreat to the line of the Somme and the Marne, with a warning thrown in that additional defence-lines had better be prepared quickly 'up to and including the *Westwall*'. He also needed every division Hitler could send him from the East.

But after the runaway Soviet summer offensive there were none to spare. Army Group Centre had been singled out for destruction in a mammoth offensive which opened on 22 June. By the end of August the Russians were on the Vistula and the Germans were fighting a full-scale battle to put down the Polish Home Army's attempt to liberate Warsaw. In the south Malinovsky and Tolbukhin crashed through the German front into Rumania, knocked Rumania out of the war, took Hitler's long-cherished Ploesti oilfield, and swept on to obtain an armistice from the Bulgarians on 2 September. As for the northern sector of the Eastern Front, Finland was out of the war and the northern Russian armies were sweeping through the Baltic states. Here a firm decision to pull right back and establish a solid front covering East Prussia could have released thirty divisions – but Hitler insisted on an inch-by-inch fight for the Baltic states. As a measure of compensation Weichs and Army Group 'E' had been ordered to pull out of Greece and Yugoslavia, with Tito's Partisans following up hard. It was utterly impossible to send a single division to the West.

By 15 September, however, a change came over the situation maps at OKW headquarters. After the devastating setbacks of the spring and summer it was obvious that the fronts were becoming stabilized. Down in Italy Kesselring and Vietinghoff had managed to fight the Allies to a halt again after their breakout from Anzio and Cassino which had taken them into Rome forty-eight hours before the D-Day landings in Normandy. On the Eastern Front the Red Army, after its nearly incredible advances since June, had clearly run out of steam. And in the West Patton had already summed up the Allied problem with his *bon mot* 'My boys can eat their belts but my tanks gotta have gas.' The pace of the advance, which had taken the Allies clean across northern France to the threshold of the Siegfried Line and the Dutch border, had ruptured the shaky supply line stretching back to the Normandy beaches. General Blaskowitz had skilfully extricated Army Group 'G' from southern France after the Allied landings in Provence on 15 August. Against all expectations, the Wehrmacht now found itself with a breathing-space.

'ONE TANK ON THE MEUSE'

The Allied attempt to deny the Wehrmacht this breathing-space
was Operation 'Market Garden', Montgomery's brainchild : an
attempt to shoot a powerful force across the lower Rhine by
sending it along a corridor pegged out across the rivers of
Holland by airborne forces. It was a worthy plan which was
deserving of better success, but the Allied planners failed to
discover that Arnhem, the northernmost target for the initial
paratroop drops, was the mustering ground for a Panzer corps
and the headquarters area of the German 1st Parachute Army
under General Student. What was even more unfortunate for
them, Model himself was in the area, scraping together troops
for a counter-attack against the Allied forces threatening
Aachen ; and when the paratroops came down at Arnhem,
virtually right into the laps of Student and Model, the German
commanders reacted very fast indeed. They managed to prevent
the 'Red Devils' from securing the all-important Arnhem
bridge, which would have guaranteed 'Market Garden' almost
certain success, and hemmed the unfortunate British paratroops
into a narrow pocket on the wrong side of the Neder Rijn. It
was a heartening victory which left the Allies with nothing
more immediately threatening than a salient protruding north
across the River Waal at Nijmegen.

Meanwhile Hitler was planning the one move the Allies –

and his own generals – believed impossible: a full-dress armoured counter-offensive to cut the Allied front in two and 'Dunkirk' its northern half.

Such an offensive was made possible because of two achievements: the economic miracle wrought by Speer, which had brought German weapon production to its peak in 1944 ; and the considerably widened call-up which had yielded over 700,000 new soldiers between August and October. With these raw materials Hitler created three new armies for his coming western venture, manned by young enthusiasts and armed magnificently (the new 'King Tiger', arguably the best tank of the war, was their Sunday punch). The operation was code-named *Wacht am Rhein* ('Watch on the Rhine'), and it was to push through the Ardennes, reach the Meuse, and drive on to Antwerp, thus cutting off Montgomery's 21st Army Group. Even more so than with *Zitadelle*, this was an all-in-one throw of the last available reserves. But, unlike *Zitadelle*, it caught the Allies completely by surprise.

On 4 September Hitler had reinstated Rundstedt as C-in-C, West, for Model had quite enough on his hands in Belgium and could no longer coordinate the crushing needs of every sector of the Western Front. When he was told the plan, Rundstedt was thoroughly sceptical and did not believe that it had a chance – but in fact Rundstedt proved to be the best 'secret weapon' the Germans employed in the Ardennes offensive. Allied intelligence reports, basing their pronouncements on Rundstedt's past record and his present age, virtually wrote off any idea of a heavy German counter-offensive. Thus the attack, when it came, was given a sharper cutting edge than it deserved because of Allied miscalculation.

Not that the cutting edge was not sharp enough as it was : nine confident new Panzer divisions, four of them SS units. Sepp Dietrich and 6th SS Panzer Army would carry the main assault, with the four SS divisions. General Hasso von Manteuffel, a veteran Panzer general from the Eastern Front, would attack in the centre. His 5th Panzer Army had three Panzer divisions. The southern flank would be carried by General Erich Brandenberger's 7th Army, whose brief was to create a 'hard shoulder' to defend the southern flank of the German corridor to the Meuse and beyond.

As D-Day – 16 December – approached, it was clear that even the most battle-hardened commander had doubts about the final outcome. Colonel Joachim Peiper, who was to lead the spearhead battle group of *Leibstandarte* in its dash for the Meuse, was given a singular briefing by Sepp Dietrich's chief-of-staff, General Krämer. 'Just make it to the Meuse . . . one tank on the Meuse, that's all I ask of you'.

Nevertheless, total surprise was gained when *Wacht am Rhein* burst upon the flimsy American front at dawn on the sixteenth. By the evening of the following day two great breaches had been opened in the American line and the Panzers were flooding through. Out in the lead was Peiper with his *Leibstandarte* battle group, heading for Malmedy, Stavelot, and the Meuse crossing at Huy. But by the twentieth three ominous bastions of resistance had fatally checked the pace of the German offensive. Peiper had got bogged down on the northern flank of the 'Bulge' and American reinforcements were preparing to seal him off in the valley of the Ambleve river. *Leibstandarte* had also run up against fierce resistance at St Vith, where an American 'horseshoe' position had taken shape. And further south, at Bastogne, Manteuffel had also been blocked by the fierce resistance of the American troops in the small town of Bastogne, forcing him to ring off the place and divert vital troops from the pounce on the Meuse crossing at Dinant. By the twenty-third the St Vith position had been evacuated but Peiper had been forced to leave all his surviving transport – immobilized for lack of fuel – at La Gleize and break out through the American ring. And Bastogne still held out. By Christmas Day Manteuffel's spearhead was within five miles of the Meuse, immobilized for want of fuel and reinforcements that were still tied down at Bastogne, when a massive American counterattack drove it back in confusion. The Ardennes offensive had reached its zenith.

It took another fortnight of hard fighting before Hitler would accept that the gamble had not come off, however, and in that fortnight the Allied air forces struck as hard as they had done in Normandy and German tank losses soared. By the time the Allies had battered the 'Bulge' flat, Hitler had once again squandered his armoured reserve.

Could the Germans have won the Battle of the Bulge ? The answer must surely be no, as witness the speed with which the Americans were able to shore up their front once the spirited defence of the Ambleve river valley, St Vith, and Bastogne had won them a breathing-space. Conversely, it is easy to see why they lost. The Panzer virtuosos had no room to manoeuvre, that essential element in the successful prosecution of armoured warfare. The narrow, snowbound roads through the Ardennes forced them to concentrate on the best roads, string out their columns, and reduce the pace to a stoppable level. Given room to manoeuvre, Manteuffel would never have dreamed of detaching such a large part of his force to ring off Bastogne. But he had no choice.

Wacht am Rhein, Hitler's last throw in the West, had failed. The initiative passed to the Allies for good, and they wasted no time in preparing for the real test : the assault on the Rhine and the break-in to the heart of the Reich.

WATCH ON THE RHINE

Eisenhower could afford to take his time about the Rhine crossing once the Ardennes venture had failed. In February and early March a triple Allied offensive – like a meat grinder with three great rollers – minced its way through the Siegfried Line and closed up to the west bank of the Rhine, the last western barrier on which the hopes of the Reich depended. Wesel, Duisburg, Düsseldorf, and Cologne marked the axes of the first advance. Bonn and Koblenz marked the second. Mainz, Worms, and Mannheim marked the third. As the Allies reached the Rhine they found bridge after bridge lying in ruins across the river, blown according to the strictest instructions from Hitler. All save one. On 7 March a motorized platoon reached the west bank of the Rhine and found to their astonishment that the massive Ludendorff railway bridge at Remagen had not been demolished and dashed in to secure it. Eisenhower had his foothold across the Rhine.

The ultimate man of method, however, he did no more than to reinforce the bridgehead and make sure that it was secure before the last German resistance on the West bank had been crushed. Not for another fortnight did he sanction the creation of new bridgeheads. Hitler had raged when he heard of the capture of the Remagen bridge. Rundstedt had been dismissed

yet again – this time for good. And in his place Hitler appointed
the man who had done wonders on the Italian front since
September 1943 : Kesselring. But there was little Kesselring
could do now. Model commanded in the Ruhr, tied down with
over 300,000 troops for the defence of the industrial heart of
the Reich. And it was Model's army group in the Ruhr that
was singled out for destruction after the main Rhine crossings
went in between 23 and 25 May. In his original plan,
Eisenhower had intended to bypass the Ruhr and drive straight
on into Germany. Now he planned to envelop it in the greatest
pincer movement ever brought off on the Western Front. The
trap was closed on 1 April and Model was sealed in the Ruhr
pocket. A breach 200 miles wide had been torn in the German
line east of the Rhine.

Model, who had always condemned Paulus for surrendering
at Stalingrad, managed to tie down eighteen American divisions
for eighteen days before the Ruhr pocket was reduced. For four
days after the surrender he was a fugitive in the ruins, alone
apart from a few staff officers. By 21 April these had all
dwindled away apart from his Intelligence chief. Finally
deciding, quite simply, that death was better than dishonour,
he asked his Intelligence chief to bury him where he was – and
shot himself. Regrettable though his suicide may seem, Model
was certainly one of the most capable and loyal generals Hitler
ever had – but he never let his loyalty deliquesce into
fanaticism.

The battle for the Ruhr pocket did not hold up the great
Allied flood eastward across Germany towards the Elbe and
Berlin. After the crossing of the Rhine there was nothing to
stop them ; by 16 April General Simpson's 9th Army had
gained a bridgehead across the Elbe.

On that day, however, the Russians finally broke through the
German defences on the Eastern Front and came surging west
towards Berlin. Eisenhower made his decision. The Allies
would stop on the Elbe.

The last hope of Hitler and his least realistic generals had
evaporated. The great rift between the Western Allies and the

Russians had failed to materialize. With his threadbare armies rapidly going under Hitler, determined to the last, prepared for a hero's death beneath the ruins of Berlin.

'NOW TAKE BERLIN!'

On 12 January 1945, the Red Army launched its own offensive into the eastern half of the Third Reich, throwing in 180 divisions – a superiority in men and tanks of six to one. By 4 February Zhukov's armies had driven through to Küstrin on the Oder – fifty miles from Berlin. But during this period the biggest battle being fought at Hitler's headquarters was not between what remained of the German army in the field and the Red Army. It was between Chief-of-Staff Guderian and Hitler.

With the bulk of the German armour still in the process of being forced back out of the Ardennes, there was no armoured reserve on the Eastern Front worthy of the name. By the twentieth the pace of the Russian offensive had accelerated to thirty-forty miles per day. Guderian pressed for the cannibalization of the former Army Group Centre and the formation of a new army group – designated 'Vistula' – to be formed from units of Army Group South. Hitler put off his decision until 25 January, turning down all Guderian's nominees for the new command – and then made what has to be the most fatuous appointment of the Second World War. He appointed Heinrich Himmler, 'Faithful Heinrich', the resoundingly-titled *Reichsführer-SS*.

At first Guderian could not believe his ears but soon found

to his horror that Hitler was in deadly earnest. The result was inevitable. Instead of getting a battle-wise commander who would know how to scrape together the biggest possible reserve, the Chief-of-Staff of the German Army got the one man totally unfitted for *any* military command, let alone the most vital sector of the front. Himmler did not know what to do and he was hustled back to the Oder in double-quick time.

However, the Russian salient was a narrow one, and Guderian planned a counter-stroke against its northern flank. It was a heavy spoiling attack, to be launched by six Panzer divisions. But Guderian had to undergo the ordeal of an appalling shouting-match before he could get Hitler to agree to the appointment of a sound staff officer, General Walther Wenck, to tell Himmler how to go about it. After screaming himself pop-eyed and purple in the face, Hitler suddenly gave way 'with his most charming smile', and agreed to Wenck's appointment. The counter-attack went in on 15 February and it had not been going forty-eight hours when Wenck got himself seriously injured in a car crash. Himmler's new chief-of-staff was General Hans Krebs, a 'Nazi general', former chief-of-staff to Model. In two more days the attack petered out and comparative peace descended over the front.

The Red Army, however, was merely busying itself with straightening out its front before the final drive on Berlin, and Guderian knew that he must get rid of Himmler before the next offensive broke. He did it by working on Himmler's own neuroses and conceit, suggesting that the overworked *Reichsführer* give up the command of Army Group Vistula. After another brief sparring match Hitler agreed and to his great relief Guderian secured the appointment on 20 March of General Gotthard Heinrici, a master at defensive tactics. All his skills would be needed now.

When Heinrici took over his first task was to superintend a limited offensive which Hitler had ordered: an attack by General Theodor Busse's 9th Army to pinch out the Russian bridgehead across the Oder at Küstrin. Heinrici found to his dismay that far too much time had been wasted: the Russians, according to their habitual practice, had built up their strength in the bridgehead until it was far too strong for Busse's forces. Heinrici's first shock came when he heard that Busse's 20th Panzer Division had been cut off by the Russians in the bridgehead. His second shock followed rapidly. Before leaving, Himmler told him that he had been negotiating for terms with the Western powers. So it was that the man who was to be the defender of Berlin took up his command : dismayed and disgusted, but determined to do his utmost to stave off the inevitable.

Heinrici's third shock came on 28 March, after Busse and the 9th Army had made repeated attempts to break through to the defenders of Küstrin. Telephoning Guderian to complain about the futility of maintaining the attack, Heinrici was astonished to hear the voice of Krebs. Guderian was gone, sacked, after a final blazing row with Hitler in which Guderian had completely lost his temper and hurled accusations at Hitler – for his absurd 'stand fast' policy in the large German towns, for his refusal to withdraw the eighteen divisions trapped in Courland, and for the totally baseless accusations the Führer never ceased to make about the Army's lack of devotion and fighting spirit. As before, Hitler calmed down suddenly, told Guderian that he needed to go on sick leave, and nominated Krebs as his successor. Hitler had dismissed the last voice of professional sanity from his Supreme Headquarters.

The storm broke on 16 April, as Zhukov and Koniev hurled their army groups across the Oder and rushed upon the scanty defence-lines of Busse's 9th Army. Like Rommel in Normandy before D-Day, Heinrici had accomplished miracles in the space of a few weeks. He was using his 'empty sack' technique, pulling back his front line just before the Russian bombardment started – a trick that needed a peculiar tactical sixth sense – and sending them back to their positions to meet the Russian assault head-on. For forty-eight incredible hours Busse's men held out along the Seelöwe Heights, stopping Zhukov dead – but to the south Koniev's forces had shattered the front held by Field-Marshal Ferdinand Schörner, a rapidly-promoted favourite of Hitler, and were streaming west at top speed. When Zhukov's forces finally broke through on the Seelöwe Heights, it was only a matter of time before Koniev came arching up from the south and surrounded Busse. Grimly, Zhukov told his commanders: 'Now take Berlin !'

By nightfall on the twentieth – Hitler's birthday – Koniev's leading troops were only eighteen miles from Berlin. The first Russian shells began to fall on the capital on the morning of the twenty-first. By the twenty-third 9th Army was surrounded – and Keitel left the deranged atmosphere of Hitler's bunker, deep beneath the New Chancellery, to fly to the headquarters of General Wenck. Barely recovered from his injuries of February, Wenck had been put in command of a 'paper army' – 12th Army – which Hitler now ordered, via Keitel, to march to the relief of Berlin. Wenck had no intention of doing any such thing ; instead he determined to do all he could to break through to Busse and get his men out to the West.

By the twenty-fifth Heinrici's command was a nightmare. His left-wing army, Manteuffel's 3rd Army, was plainly unable to hold the Oder line any longer and he ordered it to fall back. For this he was dismissed by a furious Keitel – much to his relief. It would not fall to his lot to direct the death agony of Berlin. After the twenty-seventh the three German army commanders in the Battle of Berlin were obsessed with one thing only : to get what remained of their troops out to the West. General Karl Weidling, one of Busse's corps commanders, had been given the hopeless job of co-ordinating the 'garrison' of the capital.

Forty-eight hours of nightmare ended Berlin's ordeal. Hitler shot himself in the *Führerbunker* at about 3.45 pm on 30 April. Keitel and Jodl had already left the city to carry on the fight – and to sign the unconditional surrender of the German Wehrmacht. Krebs, the last chief-of-staff of OKH, and Burgdorf, the man who had offered Rommel the choice between a People's Court and a state funeral, negotiated a cease-fire in Berlin, returned to the *Führerbunker,* and shot themselves.

In chaos and collapse, some fighting on to the last on behalf of their men, some committing suicide, some clutching the last rags of their former splendour around themselves as they surrendered, Hitler's generals finally reached the end of the road.

EPILOGUE

Basically, the story of the relations between Hitler and his generals is one of sustained paradox. He scorned them as a professional class of hidebound fuddy-duddies ; he used their talents to pull off one of the most rapid strings of amazing military conquests in the history of the world. Without the Army and its generals Hitler could never have come to power in the first place – but in the early 1930s the generals needed him as much as he needed them. Overwelmed by professional mistrust he removed, stage by stage, every vestige of independent action ever enjoyed by the German General Staff. He insulted them, humiliated them, and made his contempt for their inadequacies obvious whenever possible.

Yet above all one point stands out : he mesmerized them. He fascinated them. And he got six years of service out of them, generating genuinely sound patriotism and sense of duty out of men who as often as not loathed him and all he stood for. How he did it would form another book in itself. The fact remains unchallenged.

This study has been an attempt to show that the German military machine as modified by Hitler was more often than not an extremely Heath Robinson contraption. He had magnificent military talents on which he could call, but the personal differences among his generals meant that they did not readily work as an integrated team. In their human characteristics, Hitler's generals were as different as chalk from cheese. There was Guderian, bluff, outspoken, never afraid to shout Hitler down ; and Kluge, able, smooth, and susceptible to bribery. There was Model, the archetypal Nazi general, who nevertheless refused to let his personal loyalty to the Führer distract him from what had to be done. The list is endless ; but who can be said to have been the best of Hitler's generals ?

Four names stand out, men who always retained a sound grasp on both strategy *and* tactics : Manstein, Guderian, Rundstedt, and Kesselring. These were the élite, the men whom Hitler could never really afford to do without. Dropping the sights sharply, and trying to isolate the soundest commander at army level, Kluge's record was good throughout, despite his evasive nature and his knack of putting up the backs of his subordinates. His most serious technical flaw was the time he took to grasp the full significance of Panzer warfare. Equally excellent at army level was Model, the 'Führer's fireman', who was transferred to more totally differing fronts when the going got tough than practically any other of the generals.

What of Rommel ? He is one of the hardest of the generals to pin down. As a divisional commander of Panzer forces he is only to be compared with a general who has not featured in these pages : General Hermann Balck, the workhorse of XLVIII Panzer Corps. Rommel was slow to mature as a commander of large units. Yet his performance in Normandy before D-Day and his absolutely correct grasp of the underlying strategy to be followed gives one to wonder how he would have performed in Russia in command of an army group, the command he was expecting when Burgdorf and Maisl offered him a cyanide pill instead.

It is a pity that space does not permit any detailed treatment of the key Luftwaffe personnel, for the leading airmen of the Reich had army ranks. Such a study would single out Galland, the Guderian of the German fighter arm ; Geissler and Richtofen, competent *Fliegerkorps* commanders, and the Luftwaffe generals charged with the impossible task of defending the Reich from the Allied air raids. But the airborne forces came under Luftwaffe command, and here the two key names are Generals Kurt Student and Richard Heidrich.

It is easy to denigrate Keitel and Jodl, the yes-men of OKW. They were both capable and honest men in their way, and even Keitel was generally tolerated, if not respected. But their greatest weakness was the infection of palace politics. To get their work done they had to study Hitler's moods like amateur psychiatrists. And they were sentenced to death at Nuremberg for passing on some of the most dishonourable orders ever issued to a fighting service – the 'Commissar Order' is a case in point.

Hitler's generals were an amazingly mixed bag who achieved remarkable results despite their own differences of opinion and the totally unpredictable mind of their master. When all is said and done, that is probably the soundest epitaph they can be given.

INDEX

INDEX 163